I0212872

It's Time

5 Master Keys For Unlocking Your Family's Future

Joe McDaniel

Success In Life ®

Copyright © 2012 Joe McDaniel, Jr.
All Rights Reserved

ISBN-10: 0615508235
ISBN-13: 9780615508238

Library of Congress Control Number: 2011911667
Succes in Life Publishing, Lumberton, NC

Copyright Permission

Unless otherwise indicated, All Old Testament Scripture quotations are from The Holy Bible, English Standard Version® (ESV®), copyright © 2001 by Crossway, a publishing ministry of Good News Publishers. Used by permission. All rights reserved.

Unless otherwise indicated, All New Testament Scripture quotations are from the New Revised Standard Version Bible: Anglicized Edition, copyright 1989, 1995, Division of Christian Education of the National Council of the Churches of Christ in the United States of America. Used by permission. All rights reserved.

GOD'S WORD is a copyrighted work of God's Word to the Nations. Quotations are used by permission. Copyright 1995 by God's Word to the Nations. All rights reserved.

Some scripture quotations are from The Authorized (King James) Version. Rights in the Authorized Version in the United Kingdom are vested in the Crown. Reproduced by permission of the Crown's patentee, Cambridge University Press.

Table of Contents

Dedication

To God, from whom all blessings flow, I honor you.

This, my first book, is dedicated to my wife of two decades. Tish, you've never stopped believing in me. Thank you for your love, devotion, loyalty and faith, even when there was little reason to believe. I will forever be in your debt. You've nurtured my dreams and comforted my heart. You make life worth living. I'll cherish every single day with you.

Special thanks to my parents, the greatest parents in the world. My perpetual hope is to make you proud. Thanks for always being there when I've needed you. Regardless of age, you remove the stings of life.

To my only sister, the honor is mine; No one can take my place with you. To my nieces and nephews, all things are possible. I believe in each one of you.

To my spiritual parents, who married us and christened our children, Drs. Lonnie & Queen Sessoms, your investments and seeds of love will continue to bear fruit in us. Thank You.

To my in-laws, Wilbert & Patricia Jordan, though you gave me the most precious gift – my heart for life – you continue to give in ways too numerous to express. I am honored to be your son. Thank You.

Finally, to my four sons, Aaron, Isaiah, Caaleb and Efrim, for me, you have redefined the words life, energy, and fun. We share the joys of living, fishing, camping, golfing, and every sport that uses a ball. I love you all much more than words can express. Follow you hearts. And, wherever it leads, I'll be there.

Acknowledgements

I would like to acknowledge the following for their support and encouragement during the process of preparing this manuscript.

Dr. Eric Dent – Thanks for assisting me with balance, perspective and editorial feedback. Your heart and passion for humanity and its Creator bears much fruit.

Dr. John Hatcher – my spiritual twin brother and genuine friend – your contributions are too numerous to disclose. You are the model of manhood. Thanks for being an open book.

Pastor Mike Pittman – You have poured countless hours and hours of your life into me. Your candor and transparency are reshaping who I will become and the subsequent books that I will pin. I am eternally grateful for you.

Pastor Earl Goings – There comes a time when a bird must be released to fly and build his own family and world. Thank you for releasing me to go and to pursue my calling. You are a father's father.

Jesus Christ – there are no words to effectively articulate your role in all things. You are indeed the author and finisher.

PREFACE

This book is written for those who have struggled to find meaning in life. For those who know there is a plan for life but have not yet found it, this is for you. I've written this resource for those who have a dream, but have no idea of how to unlock that dream. For those who sometimes feel like giving up when life comes to a halt, I have you in mind. For families who are traveling the journey of life without a roadmap, I understand your journey. The following life lessons have been developed with families in mind. Whether you are young or old, rich or poor, famous or unknown, the feelings of family disorientation do not discriminate.

Through **poems, words of wisdom, philosophy and Godly advice** on many subjects that matter to you, I pray that you will find simple answers to life's tough questions in the words that follow.

Some might ask, how are you qualified to teach life lessons. My response is simple : The formula of success includes a thorough knowledge of failure. Therefore, I am uniquely qualified to help you succeed in avoiding life's toughest pitfalls. I know them all on a first-name basis. Further, I have been divinely inspired and academically trained to help you find your way. Having earned well over two hundred college credits in many subject areas and having spoken with hundreds of people about life's tough journey, I identify with all of the challenges and emotions attached with trying to find your own significance – your own path – your family's path. I've studied in the schools of John C. Maxwell, Les Brown, Pat Robertson and other key institutions around the country. By God's grace, I have gained perspective on life and how it works. Now, I am ready to return what I've learned to you. I want to help you get a handle on what matters most in life. I want to help you find your own path to success.

If you're seeking support with creating the life that you were born to live, then you will find the support you need in the **20 life lessons** that follow. I commend you for investing the time, energy and money into your own happiness.

There were places in my life where I felt nearly worthless. During those times, life had little to no value and little meaning in the grand scheme of things. Yet, through God's mercy, I later learned that I had a serial number and that no one else in life could do what I was born to do – the way I was born to do it. Just as no one else shares the exact same fingerprint or DNA, no one else has the exact same mission in life.

We are all very unique – significantly different from each other, although we may share common interests. Only you can do what you are called to do.

You are as special as the most famous superstar. The only difference between you and perhaps a superstar is that they have spent much of their lives and thousands of dollars on perfecting themselves, their gifts, who they are, their art, their product or service. You too, have meaning and something wonderful to offer the world. You must realize and believe that, in order to find the life you were born to live.

This book will provide you with the foundations to begin setting yourself and your family on course to begin unlocking your future and living the life of your dreams – the life you were born to live.

There are 5 areas that you absolutely must master in order to enjoy
the successful life you were born to live.

Master Key 1– **Education**
Master Key 2– **Career**
Master Key 3– **Finance**
Master Key 4– **Family**
Master Key 5– **Faith**

These areas are not ranked in terms of importance (Faith, being the most important) but they should help guide the development of your family's existence. These 5 Master Keys expand into 20 lessons that will unlock and reveal hidden answers to your innermost questions. The following are three such questions that will be unlocked through the contents of this book.

THE 3 MAJOR QUESTIONS

Question 1 : How do I become aware of the life that I was born to live? **Awareness**

Question 2 : How do I empower and propel myself to build my life? **Building**

Question 3 : How do I consistently maximize achievement in order to
complete my dream life successfully? **Completion**

As a result of my deep research on the "Three Major Questions", I have developed **The A,B,Cs of Dream Development**. *The 5 Master Keys,* found throughout this book, will answer the 3 major questions for developing and living your family's dreams.

A. AWARENESS

How do I become aware of the life that I was born to live?

Lessons: 1,2,3,19,20

- Who am I born to be?
- What should I be doing?
- Where should I be going?

B. BUILDING

How do I empower and propel myself to build that life?

Lessons: 4,5,6,7,8,9

- How do I prepare myself?
- How do I encourage myself?
- How do I make the first steps?

C. COMPLETION

How do I consistently maximize acheivement and complete my dream life?

Lessons: 10-18, Poems

- How do I systemize my movements?
- How do I maximize growth?
- How do I master acheivement?

Awareness

- Lesson 1: Develop Your Picture of Success
- Lesson 2: Understand Your Purpose
- Lesson 3: Discover Your Secret Road Map
- Lesson 19: Follow God's Order for Mankind
- Lesson 20: Engage the 10 Principles of Faith

Building

- Lesson 4: Master the Early Childhood Stage
- Lesson 5: Master the Elementary Stage
- Lesson 6: Master the Middle & High School Stage
- Lesson 7: Master the Collegiate Stage
- Lesson 8 10 Keys to Developing Your Career
- Lesson 9: Perfect Your Personal Performance

Completion

- Lesson 10: 3 Steps To Reaching Your Financial Goals
- Lesson 11: Unravel the Mystery of Investments
- Lesson 12: Avoid Marital Pitfalls
- Lesson 13: Set Family Ground Rules
- Lesson 14: Decide to Agree
- Lesson 15: Understand the Role of Fatherhood
- Lesson 16: Administer Positive Discipline
- Lesson 17: Pursue Good Family Entertainment
- Lesson 18: Develop Good Family Health

LIFE LESSON 1
Develop Your Picture of Success

Success. What is it? Is it millionaire status or fame? Is it a seven-letter word that we reduce only to expensive possessions, glamour and ritzy decor? I don't think so. Success is not about money or fame at all. Success is about peace. Ironically, some of the most wealthy and famous among us have very little peace. Success is peace with self and peace with God. So, what is peace? Peace is the state of wholeness, health, and harmony in every area of life. Consistently enjoying the highest level of peace with self and God means that you have developed a successful life.

> *Consistently enjoying the highest level of peace means that you have developed a successful life.*

To maintain daily peace, you must acquire self-discipline and a balanced outlook on life. We need self-discipline in order to keep us away from things that rob us of our wholeness, health, and harmony. We need a positive outlook to help push us towards the good things that our Creator has provided for us to help sustain wholeness, health, and harmony.

A successful mindset produces a successful life. This type of mindset is one that takes shape every morning to create good daily habits, which produces positive lifestyle change. Successful habits result in successful days, which result in successful years, which result in a successful life. It is important to stay on course with positive daily habits such as daily-declarations, personal affirmations, physical exercise, productivity, creativity and the fulfillment of other personal values.

> *A successful lifestyle is a daily lifestyle, which constantly moves you towards the mental photo of your life's dreams.*

Secondly, success is a journey towards a picture of a place in your mind that you've always seen, but have yet to arrive. Through your thinking, planning and positive energy, not only can you arrive at your picture of success every morning, but you can actually live there each day. Stephen R. Covey would say it this way perhaps; you should always begin your daily journey with the end in mind. The only way to successfully reach the end of your life's journey is by enjoying one successful day after another, knowing exactly where your life is headed.

A successful lifestyle is a daily lifestyle, which constantly moves you towards that mental photo of your life's dreams. It is that photo of peace, tranquility, and the complete state of resolve, which solicits your daily effort each day to pursue it. But beware. The ultimate goal is not arriving at that picture of success, but enjoying the experiences of the trip and helping others along the way.

Consider your goals and deepest dreams for a moment. Do you see a picture through your mind's eye? Describe that picture? Is it to help others in a greater way? Is it a unique accomplishment or goal?

Let's ponder the purpose of pictures for a moment. Pictures were invented to capture an event, an object or a memory. A picture allows you to revisit a scene over and over as many times as desired. Your personal success is that picture in your mind that you are constantly viewing. It will appear from time to time as you go about your affairs. And, *you will achieve that which most often consumes your thoughts.* The reason that you have that certain picture of success in your mind is because you have been created to produce that picture.

That dream or picture will come true, as you make a firm decision to walk and work toward it daily. This philosophy of daily success is found in the fulfillment that you receive through actually developing your dreams and bettering yourself each day.

The day that you firmly begin your journey towards that mental photo is actually the day that you become a success story. You must simply stay on course and enjoy each successful day after another.

Thirdly, success in life is maintaining the daily momentum and the inner resilience that keeps you firmly focused and steadily on course. It's kind of like the Wheedle Wobble that won't fall down. Punch it as often as you like; it will always snap back to quickly find its center. How resilient you really are. Success In Life is an inner peace generated from your inner compass, which is firmly locked on your destination. In short, it is unstoppable, undeniable, and unwavering.

All of creation has a destination - a specific purpose – a specific journey. You were born to grow and to move. As mobile creatures, we travel from birth to death. And, between those two points in time, there are pre-calculated stops that you must make along the way.

One of the major points of lesson one is this:

Unless you identify, calculate and declare the stops that you will make along your journey, you will travel aimlessly making stops along the way that you were never created to make. Focus on the future.

> *You were not born to live in a desert of misfortune.*

A lifestyle out of focus results in not only substantial delay, but arrival to the desert of despair and frustration. You were not born to live in a desert of misfortune.

This lesson is about declaring those calculated stops that you will make from now on. This book will teach you to intentionally travel only to those life destinations that the Creator intended to bring you peace and joy. Success is so much more than wealth and fame. It is further the enjoyment of the processes, which creates positive results in you and in those around you.

You will need these 5 master keys to achieve real success. You can attain all five keys, if you're willing to learn, explore, and work towards them. I want to help you.

You were created for a reason – a very good reason. Do you know what that reason is? You were specifically made to do something, to create something, to be something very special. What is it? The question is not what are you doing right now, or what are you creating right now or what are you being right now. The question is what "were" you made to do, what were you made to create, or what were you made to be before you were ever born.

If you were like me ten years ago, you may simply not know the answers to those questions. You can find those answers, if you search deeply within. Take a few moments, perhaps a few days to develop your picture of success in the dark room of your mind. Explore whom you really are and what you need to do to become the person you are within. When you discover yourself, then embrace yourself and never let you go.

It's Time to develop the successful inner you.

Change who you are on the inside and you change your experience with life on the outside. Normally, we use negatives to develop pictures. But, from now on, use positives to develop your new life. Use positive inner talk of who you were born to be and who you will become. Turn your negatives into positives. Develop yourself with positive daily words – out loud. Tell yourself who you will become. You will soon find that your positive inner talk in the dark room of your photographical mind will soon become reality. Take a few moments to complete the workbook for Lesson 1.

LIFE LESSON 2
Understand Your Purpose

Every tool is created for a purpose - created to solve a problem. Let's examine a tool – the screwdriver, for example. As helpful as this tool is, it is very easy to overlook the creator of the screwdriver and go on to use this tool without ever considering the designer – its creator. Who stops to ever appreciate the inventor of the screwdriver? Who even knows the inventor's name? If I were to ask you, who invented the light bulb, you would likely reply, Thomas Edison, of course. Now, who invented you?

Always remember that you are also a tool made by a designer – your Creator. You were created for a purpose. Here's another question for you. How often have you, the tool, been used for the purpose for which you were created? You see, ***existence void of purposeful awareness is the story of frustrated lives.***

Let's consider another tool – the hammer, for example. Imagine a hammer being used as a wrench. What is the result? Poor success, you're correct. No harmony at all. Imagine a car being used as a garbage truck. What is the result? Very poor success – correct again. That would be unhealthy for the car. Cars are not made to carry tons of trash and neither were you. You cannot be successful operating outside of your designer's intentions.

Here lies the problem of far too many lives. As astonishing as it sounds, very few people are doing what they were born and created by God to do. Anecdotally, we know that the average employment span of an employee is between 2 and 4 years, before they move on to a new job. In addition, we know that those employees are often unhappy doing what they're doing. In fact, many retire from professions and are still unhappy with life even after retirement.

The reason for this is because your purpose never ends at retirement. Your purpose is for life. Many never find their purpose in life; therefore, many never realize any real and lasting success – or peace with themselves. Because, success is NOT

> *.....success is NOT merely having wealth for retirement; it is in knowing that you have fulfilled the intent for which you were born.*

merely having wealth for retirement; it is in knowing that you have fulfilled the intent for which you were born. This is unity with self and unity with your Creator. ***Enjoyment with life is a sign that you may have found purpose in life.***

Here's another question: What brings you joy and fulfillment? What could you do forever for other people? Real success is never totally about you. Remember, as a tool, *you were created to solve a problem for others and to bring enjoyment to someone else first.* As a result of helping others find enjoyment, you find your own peace and enjoyment. Most people are looking for a career to help pay bills versus a lifestyle of enjoyment, which simultaneously meets the needs of others. ***Your lifestyle of success begins with finding and understanding your purpose.***

> *Your purpose is often very near you and sometimes you must withdraw from your daily routine to notice it.*

My father retired as a knitting mechanic after 33 years with the same company. And, though he commuted an hour everyday to work, he worked out of commitment, not enjoyment. Ironically, the only thing he ever truly enjoyed was being self-employed. You see, every evening after work and on week-ends, he would work for himself, in his own small business. Every Saturday, for 33 years, he would operate his little business apart from his primary profession. Consider this : Very often, one's purpose and one's profession are not the same, though they should be the same. The two were not aligned for my father. Imagine that after 33 years of dedication and commitment, hardly missing a day of work from his employer, my dad's purpose and yearning was always to be self-employed! Dad loved serving customers in his own special way. He enjoyed helping the community and putting smiles on the faces of his long-time customers. Your purpose is often very near you and sometimes you must withdraw from your daily routine and give notice to what brings you joy and happiness.

I suppose that had my father been self-employed with the same degree of dedication that he provided his employer for 33 years, he would have experienced a very different life. At least, he would have enjoyed more years of his dream job, all while providing for himself and his family. As a young man, I once asked my father, why he had this little weekend business on the side. He replied, "I enjoy it; I enjoy helping people".

Today, after retirement, my father has chosen to rest every day, in his own small business. It's been nearly 50 years now and his response is still the same. "I enjoy helping people". He has found peace and enjoyment in helping people.

I find this ironic little story quite common among many. It seems that we're born to do one thing and spending a lifetime doing another. Let me tell you, it doesn't have to be that way. I encourage you to embrace the steering wheel of your life and take a right - a right turn towards your life's destination!

You may be asking, "Well………how am I going to do that and just how do I determine what I'm created to do?" Here's the answer in a riddle. The tool cannot define itself. ***You cannot define your own identity.*** Only the one who creates the tool knows it function and knows its path. Ask your Creator to reveal your purpose in life, your place of peace with self and with Him - your place of Success In Life.

Like others, you may be asking an additional question; "Will my Creator respond to me; does He talk back?" I believe that our Creator communicates with us in ways that we're most comfortable. I believe that God communicates with us subtly, yet mysteriously through our own being and thoughts.

For example, has a light bulb ever come on inside you, to the point that you've said out loud, "that's it!", or "I've got it!", or "I see it!" Have you ever run across something in your mind that brings a sense of closure or perfect resolution to a question or dilemma you've pondered? Sure you have; we all have. I believe that our Creator often communicates with us in instances just like this. At other times, an inspiration or answer may come through reading or speaking to someone or observing others in a similar situation.

You may have seen someone doing something and said to yourself, I think I would like to do that. Perhaps, there's a dream embedded deeply inside you, which occasionally speaks from within as you observe others doing something of interest.

Let's use one final analogy here in lesson 2. Consider the screwdriver – a brand new unused screwdriver – still in the pack. And, for demonstration, we'll animate this tool and bring it to life. Until its first use, the screwdriver is probably asking itself several things (in our world of imagination). It may be asking itself, why am I here, in the midst of other things that look very differently than I? Why was I created? Consider those possible imaginary thoughts of a new unused screwdriver. Imagine, before its initial use, it may be saying to itself, "I have no purpose". "I am unfulfilled, I have no function".

These are questions that you may have rehearsed at some point in your life. This early stage of life and questioning can be very difficult. In fact, one can spend decades asking themselves the question, "why am I here".

We are the story of the screwdriver, until we suddenly find ourselves upon a screw for the very first time. All of the sudden, "There it is. I fit something perfectly. I was born for this. I was made for this screw; I AM a screwdriver; I just know it; It feels right! This has to be; it's so comfortable and natural for me. I now know who I am and what I'm supposed to do!

If you have never had that moment, expect it. What a great feeling it is? The Ah Ha moment is what it is sometimes called. It's the moment where you capture a divine glimpse of your inner self and your destined journey. It is the place of peace (resolution) with self and peace (resolution) with your Creator. It's the moment when you realize who and what you are. It's a brief moment in eternity when you experience inner closure about your purpose in life.

Seeing through God's eyes for even a tiny second can change the course of your entire life and the generation after you.

> *This book is a resource which allows you to discover, embrace and assemble your picturesque road map to Success In Life, together with me, your Personal Life Consultant.*

These moments and glimpses of life are like getting a major piece to life's puzzle. Now, I have bad news and I have some additional good news for you. Bad news first: You have already discovered many of the pieces to life's puzzle. And, you have probably lost most of those pieces if not all of them. Not knowing what those Ah Hah moments really were, you were not able to effectively capture them for your life's journey.

But, there is good news. Ah Hah moments always return to those who will gratefully embrace them. Oftentimes, to find something you were never seeking is void. But, to find that which completes your inner search of self is absolutely exhilarating.

This book is an excursion - a personal get-away, written to help you discover, embrace and assemble your pictorial map to Success In Life. I will be your personal tour guide – a Personal Life Consultant. We'll learn to notice and to capture those mental pictures. We'll learn to value those "Ah hah moments" which will become landmarks on your map to Success In Life.

Throughout the book, you should take opportunities to record your discoveries about yourself and your journey towards peace and success. By the end of the book, you should have a complete road map to life. You will have a roadmap to Success In Life. This book should serve as a tangible reference guide for you and your family for many years to come. **It's Time to begin operating in your purpose.** Congratulations on taking, perhaps, the most significant step of your life. Take a few moments to complete the workbook for Lesson 2.

LIFE LESSON 3
Discover Your Secret Road Map

A s I've discussed the contents of this book with friends and family, certain comments would often arise, such as: "We were never taught about these things, or no one ever told us about that, or we would have done better about education, finance, and marriage, if only someone had taught us about these things from the very beginning. Hence, this book is about full disclosure on 5 of the most critical topics that you'll ever face as a human being, while on your journey towards daily success.

Success In Life is not a destination; it is a predetermined route - a journey. Your first step in discovering success is to discover the route. Once the route is discovered, the next objective is to locate where you are on the route.

As an amateur golfer, I'm never interested in getting to the 18th hole - the end of the course. On the contrary, my primary goal is to enjoy the challenge of every swing. It is to enjoy the beautiful scenery of every tee and every hole. To me, being an amateur golfer does not require that I master the entire course – certainly not all at once. I only need to know a couple things to enjoy the experience of golfing. I need to know the fundamentals of a good golf swing and how to correct my swing when I make errors. I also need to know exactly where I am in relation to the hole and the direction and distance that my swing should accommodate.

> *True success in life allows you to enjoy the trip much more than the destination.*

The entire course consists of 18 stops and several swings for each hole. My purpose with golf is not to be Tiger Woods or Phil Mickelson, but to be me, and to enjoy the entire course – no matter how long it takes – usually three to four hours. During that course of time, I enjoy friendship, time with my sons, the peace of nature, the lessons learned about my game, and the lessons of those I'm playing with.

You see, true Success In Life allows you to enjoy the entire trip much more than the destination.

> *You must know where you are going or you'll spend a lifetime traveling to a very popular place called nowhere.*

This book will assist you with mapping the route to your place of peace with The 5 Master Keys of Life: **Education, Career, Finance, Family, and Faith**.

At this point, you need to make a decision. Make an absolute decision to fully write out your course for life, using this book as a resource. Instead of riding in the back seat of a car going anywhere, use this book of life lessons and wisdom to command your stirring wheel of life. You must know where you're going or you'll spend a lifetime traveling to a very popular place called nowhere.

> *Success in life doesn't mean that you've found the perfect life; it means that you've found a way to successfully handle life's imperfections, ...*

It is absolutely up to you to choose to discover the secret roadmap to your journey of success. Consider your legacy. Consider those who are waiting for you to fund their college expenses. Consider having a life that meets your choices versus a life that meets other's demands. You deserve to be completely you. Your family deserves the best "you" that you can produce. Don't cheat yourself by giving up on your dreams. Don't cheat your family by giving up on your dreams. Your creator did not make you a failure. You determine the fulfillment of your success story - a complete story from beginning to end. Write for yourself a new chapter in life in a new direction.

Failure is a choice. Success is also a choice. Success In Life doesn't mean that you've found the perfect life; it means that you have found a way to successfully correct life's imperfections, while choosing to stay on course. Allow me to share my purpose with you. My purpose in life is "Helping You Enjoy Life". That's my journey which has been partially mapped out through writing this book. I want to help you enjoy life.

<u>It's Time</u> for you to take a right turn towards the life of your dreams. The light is green; what direction will you choose?

MASTER KEY 1
Become An Educational Leader

Education is the perpetual force of development which compels one to become an asset to one's self and others. It is a position of formation and life-long learning. In our society, we are not always recognized for how well we know a subject. Rather, we are recognized by our credentials, which prove a certain level of knowledge and understanding of a subject. We have somehow misconstrued the beauty of life-long learning by devaluing learning when it does not lead to a diploma or credential. This position on training may have veered a bit too far into testing and credentialing instead of nurturing, development and performance.

Education should never be about status, but rather the trained ability to take action; it should never be used as a social throne, but rather a social calling to serve mankind. Education is about leading the generations to a deeper level of understanding about life and the potential contributions one should make to it. Education enables us to go farther than we could have gone without it; it enables us to reach higher than we could have reached before. Education allows us to empower the world - the world of our minds - even when resources are limited.

> *Education is about leading the generations to a deeper level of understanding about life and the potential contributions one should make to it.*

When learning and development are strained, one's capacity to lead future generations is severely minimized. From pre-school to college, formal education requires more than 20 years on a fulltime basis. According to the latest statistics, secondary education in the U.S. significantly lags international competitors. Why? It is because we arrive late and leave early.

Learning should begin in the womb and continue throughout the afterlife, if that were possible. The truth is that significant learning should forever be integrated throughout our daily lifestyles. Yet, we are traditionally allowed to check-out of learning at ages 18 and 22 or so, as if we are fully prepared to survive global competition and changing job markets.

A 20-year process of educational development is not nearly enough time to advance a generation. So, this begs the question. How then do we make the quantum leap forward, when we have abandoned learning and allowed our children and young adults to become exceedingly more fascinated with athletes and entertainers than scientists and entrepreneurs?

We make this leap forward by building educational momentum, which passes our personal achievements down to our children and our grandchildren. Absolutely, we must first possess educational advancements before we can pass them down. Education is the family heirloom that has been lost.

Many of our children have become disinterested with learning because we have become disinterested with learning and more consumed with life. We have turned to lifestyles of entertainment - engaged in Hollywood based glamour instead of research, innovation, and intellectual empowerment. We have exchanged college funds and SAT workshops for new cars and fancy possessions. We spend more money on vacations to Disney than we spend investing time in the local library, museum, historical sites, or trade shows.

Why are we lagging educationally? Perhaps, we have lost sight of our founding values? Perhaps, we have lost our fascination with the Creator of the universe, science, math, and philosophy? Maybe, we have laid the responsibility of education solely on our teachers and not ourselves, as parents and opinion leaders? Some would say, we are no longer investing in ourselves. As a result, we have coached our children into educational bankruptcy?

Whatever the reason, only one term will lead us out of this dilemma. That term is the word "change". We must change our course and perception on education immediately, if we will advance ourselves and save our generations. We must force ourselves to raise the bar of expectations, while fixing our sights on new horizons and new solutions.

Some might ask, does it truly require more than 20 years of learning to survive and to compete in a global society, or has the quality of our k-12 education somehow grown less effective? Others may ask, has our children's ability to absorb diminished? My answer is this. Through my observations as a consultant, professor, and thinker, the answer resides in the emphasis that American households place upon the quality and importance of education.

When we rate the importance of education by our own individual actions, many of us may score poorly. Remember, education (in my own words) is a perpetual force of development, which compels one to become a better asset to themselves and others. In other words, learning is growing; learning is investing – investing the time and effort to know more. Rate the importance that you place on education by asking yourself, am I developing and growing or merely existing? Am I spending my money on something that is alive or on objects that have virtually expired with very low residual value?

> *When we lose sight on how to achieve peace and quality of life, we put our children at risk of inheriting the same disposition.*

The importance of education is found in your quality of life. Education directly links us to a certain quality of life – not necessarily a certain income, but a quality of life, which eventually leads us to peace with ourselves. Are you happy with what you have become? If so, that's wonderful. If not, you must commit to learning more about you, about life, about the world, about your career, about what makes you happy and what brings you peace.

When we lose sight on how to achieve peace and quality of life, we put our children at risk of inheriting the same disposition. This state of confusion subsequently threatens the well-being of our educational systems, neighborhoods – even our country. How, you may ask? Our children inherit our disposition of confusion when we tolerate lower salaries for teachers and fewer resources for students. When we neglect the right to vote and to make our voices heard by not attending school board meetings, we become the problem instead of the solution. When we elect legislators who trade in higher learning outcomes for their lack of interest, time, patience, energy, and persistence to solve our educational and generational challenges, we, as a result, foster generational ignorance.

It's a vicious cycle stemming from what we all have become internally – less focused on tomorrow and more focused on today.

Shall we now lead the charge of educational expectations rather than allow governments and school systems to bear the burden of expectations alone? As citizens, elected officials, and home builders, we collectively set the expectations for our country, our community, our homes.

As it relates to our children, they often have poor examples of educational leadership, but we can change this by leading them in a new direction. Lead by example. Ask yourself this question: What example are you setting for your children and grandchildren? What do you subtly encourage them to do through your own educational actions or lack thereof? I realize that my words may be a bit strong. But, we must become more involved and become better examples. No, it's not comfortable, but we must show them the way, and not only point the way. We must first become inspired to make a difference before we can expect them to follow. Allow me to provide a little more direction on how we change for the better.

> *As it relates to our children, they often have poor examples of educational leadership, but we can change this by leading them in a new direction.*
> *Lead by example.*

Education is a culture that we involuntarily create.

Whether we intend to or not, we create an educational model by what we've already accomplished and through what we're currently accomplishing educationally. Like it or not, you are the mold in someone's eyes. The books you are seen reading today, the conferences you are seen attending tomorrow, the teachers you are seen supporting this year, and the homework you are seen grading creates an educational culture in your home. You are indeed the example of educational perfection that someone near you will inevitably adopt. And, the only one who can change your model on education is you.

Now, by acquiring education, you may assume that I mean acquiring a bachelor's degree or a PhD. Absolutely not. What I am suggesting is that you create an educational culture - a model of education - even if you haven't completed high school. It is not your diploma, but your disposition on education, which dictates your development, decisions and actions. Therefore, you must re-examine your educational intentions and consider changing the model you are presenting to those around you.

By definition, education is the act of acquiring knowledge, right? You may acquire knowledge formally or informally. In other words, learning is not exclusive to a classroom. We customarily refer to formal education as grammar school, high school, and college. We refer to informal education as acquiring know-how, on-the-job training, or picking up a trade of some kind.

Consider this. One may know how to successful run a business and not know how to read. I've met these success stories occasionally and you may have too. From owners of city dry cleaners to neighborhood mechanic shops to owners of fueling stations, I have witnessed many perform very well in business without formal education. However, if you're able to master both formal education and informal education, you provide a sense of security, value, and advancement for yourself, your family and your customers that will pay much higher dividends for generations to come.

Statistically speaking, the higher your formal education, the higher your income. That's just a fact.

We all know, the more know-how you have, the more potential you have for creating and increasing income. Notice, I did not say creating wealth, but creating income. The ability to create income and the ability to create wealth are two different abilities. From an accounting standpoint, one can have significant income creating ability and yet be virtually poor in terms of net worth. We'll further discuss wealth building in Master Key 3, Pursuing Financial Health.

The intent of the heart always leaves a trail. If you're investing your money and time in education, it simply shows.

Education, whether formal or informal, provides the ability to create income when mixed with shrewd innovation and solid decision-making. My grandfather called this concept "book smarts" versus "common sense". You have likely heard this colloquialism as well. This mixture of both is very important in the game of life. Common sense or basic intuition will take you far in life, but common sense when mixed with book smarts will enable you to take more people with you. Much of my life, I have had neither common sense nor book smarts. "To thine own self be true", Shakespeare once said. Examine where you are and evaluate your decisions on learning and your position on education. **Before you can change the future, you must acknowledge the present.**

Before you can change the future, you must acknowledge the present.

I've asked the question, why do we place so little value on education? The responses are usually, "But, we do place high value on education". Where is the evidence, I often think?

As your personal life consultant, let's take a quick survey to determine the levels of value you place upon education. Give yourself one point for each question. Let's begin.

1. Do you spend money annually on educational products – books, tapes, or educational resources? If so, how much?
2. Do you contribute to your children's or your grandchildren's college fund?
3. Do you attend parent/teacher meetings concerning your children, grandchildren, nieces or nephews?
4. Do you personally attend self-help conferences and/or seminars for which you actually pay?

Now, tally your score. How well did you do? 1,2,3, or 4 points? You've heard the wise biblical saying, "where your treasures are, your heart will be also". The evidence of our heart is found in the money trail, the time trail, and the attention trail. The intent of your heart always leaves a money trail. If you're adequately investing your money and time in education, it simply shows. Here is a little good news. You get 1 point for investing in this book.

Now, don't only consider yourself while reading this book, also consider others while reading. What more can you do to foster learning? There are others who need to join you in a group study of the principles of this book. Remember, there is a 16-week study guide, which is available to assist you, your family, and friends. Pass it on and make a difference, in your family, church, community, or organization.

I want to encourage you to continue the pursuit of educational success.

At Success In Life Ministries, we're committed to assisting you in any way that we can, through speaking, training, or one-one-one consulting. Now, back to the subject. Ask yourself. Do I really…. really…. have a heart for education? Ask yourself right now, out loud. Should I have a greater heart for education? If the answer is yes, then, congratulations, we can help you. And, it should not take very long. Simply take a moment. Put the book down for a little while, and make a commitment to simply do more. Think about things that you can do to affect change.

Consider your educational culture and what adjustments you can make. Declare to yourself, I will not only make a difference, I will be the difference. Take a moment and decide whether you're ready to take that next step to becoming an educational influence for yourself and those around you. Think about that for a few minutes and we'll pick up here a little later.

Take A Pause

Congratulations on taking the next step. "**It's Time**" to raise the bar on education. This is how we'll begin. Say, the following statement out loud. "I am a life-long learner". Say it once more, "I am a life-long learner". Now, don't be afraid to tell others who you are. You are now a life-long learner. This means that learning is now a part of your genetic fabric. Wherever you go, it's very important that you create a culture and an environment for yourself and those around you that fosters learning. This is the 1st master key for unlocking successful living. Become an educational leader in your area, home or business and create a perpetual environment for learning. You are the force for development.

Create a habitat for yourself, which includes <u>purchasing</u> positive books, CDs, DVDs. No one plants a seed without soil, fertilizer or at least water. Grow yourself and those around you. Consider creating a personal journal for your educational observations, goals and dreams. You'll find that learning is one of the most fascinating life skills you'll ever possess.

Through this process of developing your environment and increasing your appetite for learning, you'll begin to create a new culture in your home and in your community. This exciting culture of self-empowerment is actually what is missing with our current generations, in my humble opinion; we must foster a new culture for personal growth and development. Today, we predominately have a culture of fun and excitement (games, gadgets and videos) rather than a culture of family-based exploration and healthy development. Together, we can change our culture from games, gadgets and videos to one of discovery, industry, and ingenuity.

Today, we predominantly have a culture of entertainment rather a culture of home-based exploration and development.

Remember, a few decades ago, when spelling bees, recitals and trivia contests were our entertainment in our churches, schools and community centers? Our country at that time had a greater appetite for advancement through learning. Learning was exciting during those times. However, our appetites have since become overly saturated with party life, ball games, Hollywood, and popular superstars, which presents a false reality to most of us. Today, reading, puzzles, and word games are no longer on our family's agenda. Science fairs, aquariums, museums, and business seminars are not nearly as popular today as the shopping mall, which is design to reduce your net worth instead of increase it.

Remember when we were asked, "what do you want to be when you grow up"? We would say.... doctor, lawyer, and teacher, right. Today, the answers are actor, singer, and dancer. And, while these are all great professions, these entertainment-based professions are desired because we have not shown ourselves or our children that we can be wealthy through inventions, research, investments, and entrepreneurship. When we honor our entertainment-based professions with extraordinarily high salaries and allow teachers to live paycheck to paycheck, we inadvertently shift the value systems toward entertainment rather than personal learning and development. In essence, we encourage our children to follow the money, instead of following their hearts, which will lead to both happiness and financial reward.

There is a degenerative and yet contagious culture today, which subtly opposes progressive learning and promotes high-impact pop-culture and ill-gotten riches. Needless to say, we can either lead our homes back to learning-based cultures or be led by other countries and big industries seeking our paychecks through the purchase of their gaming products, sneakers, high-dollar clothing, cell phones, gadgets and star-struck entertainment.

Learning is not something that only occurs in a classroom. Rather, learning should be an intentional culture that develops in the home. Learning must be exciting. We must make learning exciting, just as we make anything else exciting. If you will not choose to make learning **fun** and **important** to your family, who will?

America is a great country, but it became great through faith and courage, through the pursuit of dreams and exploration, invention, and industrialism. The car, the airplane, the space ship were all significantly advanced here in the U.S.A. The skyscraper, the light bulb, the personal computer, and the robot were all made or advanced right here in good ole U. S. of A. To me, whether it's actually true or not, America is the country of firsts; a country of significant advancements. However, doesn't it seem that we're not as fascinated with technology and industry? Our global positioning on invention and advancement is waning. A country so young, so powerful, and so passionate about learning and exploration is seemingly taking the lead in crime, drugs, high school drop-outs, social immorality, political buffoonery, and economic disaster. Are we slipping as a nation? Have we become disoriented with what's important?

When we see high school dropouts growing and at an all time high, we must inspect the status quo. We're witnessing low college retention and struggling college graduation rates. We're seeing extremely high college debt and little to no college savings. We must take action in creating a better culture and better outcome for education.

The greatest form of progress begins with self-confrontation. Let's confront ourselves, before we confront our school boards and our teachers. Let us confront the educational time and attention that we invest in our small children, our adult children and ourselves before we point the finger at the government. We've created and elected our government to support our nation's academic affairs. However, the full responsibility of education in your home is yours.

> *The greatest form of progress begins with self-confrontation.*

When self-confrontation occurs, we inevitably make progress from the bottom up.

Consider the following actions needed for educational change:
- Take time to tutor children – anyone's children. Volunteer your time.
- Seek to build educational networks within your communities.
- Inspect the hearts of parents and children around you.
- Seek to be the difference between responsibility and educational irresponsibility.

Together, we can change the educational culture in our communities.

I have found my profession in higher education a most rewarding calling. To see the enlightened faces and corrected postures of college students I teach is very fulfilling. Knowing that I have affected the next generation's income, lifestyle, and career is very gratifying. I believe that you will also find great reward in developing the most powerful resource given to man – the mind.

There are specific levels of education for which I'd like to offer continued support in the words that follow, beginning with early childhood and ending with graduate school. Join me, as we further explore education – the first master key to unlocking your family's future.

Pearls In The Sea

Education is not only knowing what to do, but yielding every equity of sweat.
It is an opportunity that few relentlessly embrace and many leave to regret.

It has the power to change a nation, even the power to change the world.
Education must be pursued, to the depths of the sea, for there you'll find her true pearl.

Whether you're young or whether you're old, never leave to the next generation to find.
For what they possess already are pearls in the sea - the ability to explore the mind.

- Joe McDaniel

Life Lesson 4
Master the Early Childhood Stage

Whether you know it or not, the early childhood years are the *most important* years in the development of a child's educational life. Early childhood education is like the foundation to a building. I suppose we may think first grade through fifth grade are the most critical years, but it's actually the earlier years – pre-school. Ages zero to five are the most important foundational years of a child's development. Very young children consume more, grow more brain cells, and make more cognitive connections during this period than in any other period in their lives.

> *Early childhood education is like the foundation to a building.*

Consider the construction of a building. The concrete or foundation is laid first before one begins to construct a building. This is to say that ages zero to five are the concrete or foundation of a child's life. These are the years that they gain fundamental orientations about life and learning. These years set the stage and appetite for learning. By first through third grades, usually negative educational cultures will have already come to challenge any positive momentum. We have the power to promote and foster life-long learning in these early years. In fact, it's our responsibility to do so.

Have you ever heard of musical protégés, who can play classical music at ages three, four, and five? This type of phenomenon speaks to the appetite for learning at early ages. On the other hand, try learning classical compositions at thirty, forty or fifty. It simply doesn't absorb as easily, it seems.

The human brain can be pushed more aggressively at ages two, three, and four than at any other point in life.

So, what do we teach our children from zero to five? Well, most often not very much. We inadvertently underestimate the child's capacity to absorb because the child is not able to fluently articulate. However, young children can absorb much quicker than they can articulate and respond at those ages. In addition, we teach our children very little because we assume that they can only handle little.

I once saw a young child, whose father was a mathematician, solve mathematical equations that were seemingly a mile long on a college chalk board. The child couldn't have been more than four or five years of age. In fact, the child could do mathematical equations better than he could speak – being so young. Because of a parent's lack of fear, a virtual toddler can now pass a college calculus exam. Therefore, we must accept that your children, nieces and nephews can do the same, if we had more capacity and patience to teach them and push them. It takes incredible initiative and concern about the development of a child's dream and potential in order to take the needed actions to affect them and their generation. Your educational acumen will be made evident by your child's educational accomplishments.

A child will naturally excel when an environment of learning is fostered.

How do we find a place of peace and fulfillment in the area of early childhood education? The parent holds the child's key to success, even at the age of zero. What decisions will you make about your infant's education, or your toddler's education, or the toddlers of your neighborhood? Please bear in mind that as a community and a nation, we are collectively responsible for our infants and toddlers. We all have infants and toddlers in our community; and we all must take an active role in ensuring that our children will experience the most aggressive learning opportunities, while brain development is at its peak.

The following are five things that we can do to ensure that our infants and toddlers have a strong foundation.

1. Read to our children, even if they don't understand the words we're reading. Reading advances their vocabulary more quickly and increases their desire to learn.
2. Make their bedrooms vibrant, colorful, well lit, visually stimulating, and fully stocked with exciting tools that promote learning and not only entertainment and pastime.
3. If your child is in daycare, meet with their pre-school teachers on a weekly to bi-monthly basis to determine how to continue their learning and development while at home. Once again, very young children learn rapidly because of their rapid brain growth and their special ability to absorb. Keep pace with their appetite to learn.
4. Though children enjoy playing freely, ensure that their playing has purpose. Look for opportunities to teach them while they play. Make learning fun. Watch them explore and support their exploration with teachable moments.
5. Don't speak baby gibberish to infants and toddlers; speak fluent English. This replicated gibberish creates distorted speech, delayed learning, and limited vocabulary. Jump-start their reading and comprehension by exposing them to good English.
6. Begin introducing your toddlers to personal computers and learning-based software rather than video games and other intense high-impact entertainment. Early and excessive exposure to this makes normal life functions boring to them (i.e. reading and classroom attention) and

recalibrates or shortens normal attention spans. In some cases, I believe that children have been inadvertently diagnosed with attention deficit disorder - ADD.

7. Most importantly, limit television and extraneous web browsing, YouTube, etc. for all ages, as miscellaneous TV competes with the independence needed for reading time, personal growth and exploration. As long as the television is constantly powered on, an artist

Children will become what you expose them to.

cannot be developed - nor a scientist, architect, mathematician, veterinarian, or physician. The reason that our children want to be movie stars, ball players, and performers more than anything is because that's who they study from the crib through college, via television. Regardless of age, all children will aspire to become what you expose them to. Instead of excessive tele-vision, give them another vision, a vision of who they can become. Instead of exposing young children to violence and the lewd cultures found in 21st century video, expose them to strong examples of what they were born to become.

Zig Ziglar once said, "The two most important days of your life are 1) the day you were born and 2) the day you know why". Through my anecdotal research, I've come to accept that children are given the gift of **why** they are born, sometime after the close of this early childhood phase. As guardians, we must help them and support them on this journey to why. Further, this purposeful support is not necessarily provided by simply asking the popular question, what do you want to be when you grow up, but rather exposing them to the varieties of life and studying their inclinations. Somewhere in the process, you will hear, "I want to do that".

Once again, good entertainment is great, but it generally does not advance the child's future endeavors. Entertainment is not what advances nations, ideologies, and communities, but rather the equipped and prepared generations are what advance our world. In order to further global leadership, industrialization and innovation, we must further our commitment to prepare our offspring. Take a few moments to complete the workbook for Lesson 4.

LIFE LESSON 5
Master the Elementary Stage

Elementary education, as you know, is considered to be grades kindergarten through five. While early childhood focuses on brain development, elementary education focuses on basic subject development – the three R's - reading, writing, arithmetic, and other introductory subjects. Students acquire a common body of knowledge, which they will need to build upon in the later grades.

> *It's important to remember that in these years of subject development, learning styles must be determined and supported.*

It's important to remember that during these years of subject development, learning styles must be determined and supported. Please allow me to expand on learning styles. Just as you have a favorite color, or favorite hobby, you also have a favorite method for learning. Some may prefer to see things demonstrated, while others prefer pictures when learning. Others may prefer hands on or interactive learning, while others prefer to listen attentively to a teacher or instructor. There are other detailed variations of these styles, but these are the basics. Most teachers are familiar with learning styles and you should also be familiar with them. Know your own preferred learning style, as well as your children's preferred learning style.

It is in the elementary years when learning challenges begin to surface. When they surface, it is absolutely critical that you quickly capture your child's learning style and provide ample support for their growth and development. Unless there is a strong learning disability, most children should be making proper grades. However, every child will not make the grade because of various challenges, which include learning challenges, domestic challenges, emotional challenges, and personality challenges.

Personality has a lot to do with educational development during the elementary years.

As children are developing subject knowledge, they are also developing their personalities. This is where a child's friends, habits, and exposure begin to shape how they will learn and actually perform in school. It is absolutely critical that you safeguard your child from unhealthy influences, habits, and exposure, as they can quickly set patterns of poor performance and resentment against school and learning. If this occurs, the challenge of getting your child back on track could be very difficult.

Learning By Personality

Allow me to expand on personality a little more. In several models that I've studied, I've discovered 5 basic personality types – In my own words, they are the following: **the leader, the charismatic, the reserved, the analytical, and the artistic.** In other words, I have further named them **the boss, the movie star, the turtle, the Einstein and the artist**, respectively.

It is important to know which personality your child has, as everything they do (including learning) will manifest in some way through their personality. Why is this important to know? This is important because parents and teachers OR teachers and students may have conflicting personalities which could be counterproductive as far as learning is concerned. Not understanding these nuances can create vacuums in communication, and consequently challenge learning.

If a child is a bossy child, who likes to learn quickly, and the instructor prefers a slow methodical approach, then there could be a challenge with learning, unless the instructor is able to make adjustments based upon the student's individual personality and preference. Or, if a child has an analytical personality but has a movie star for a teacher or parent, then there could be silent frustrations with learning, unless there is some form of compromise that accommodates the learner.

> *For maximum educational consumption, children must learn in a format which best suits their individual needs.*

For maximum educational consumption, children should learn in a format that best suits their individual needs. However, that's not very practical in our large traditional classrooms. No classroom is filled with children who all wear the same shoe size. Likewise, all children think, process, and learn differently from each other. It may be very difficult for a child to excel when they're in a room with various other learning personalities and a teacher who also has an incompatible teaching style.

Out of fairness to teachers, most are trained in these types of social dynamics regarding developmental learning. However, a child may be significantly disadvantaged when social dynamics are not well understood. A child suffering with these challenges may not be able to articulate what is occurring.

An involved parent will detect these challenges, through observing academic performance and the child's behavior toward learning. You may in fact notice the following statements. "I don't like that class", or "I don't understand my homework", or they may say, "it's boring" or "the teacher goes too fast". These are all signs that there may be a social mismatch in the learning experience. In other words, the learning process should not be a one size fit all. That is to say that children are not robots that can be programmed to function the same way at the exact same pace. Teachers and most importantly parents must be able to adjust the pedagogy for their child's learning style, especially if academic performance begins to drastically decline.

For a teacher to say, "well, all the other children.......are doing fine in this area" is a statement of poor compromise. Again, all children are not alike. Each student will excel in their subject of dominance. Let's examine the five personalities individually.

The Boss personality generally prefers learning that is quick, concise, and to the point. They want it quick and straight to the point. They basically get it, and are quickly bored when instruction is prolonged in their opinion. They may easily become distracted or they may become distractions to others when instruction is drawn-out or seemingly pointless to them. To this personality group, everything must be quick, clean, and to the point. For teachers, I would suggest pulling this group aside to perhaps satisfy their quicker pace with additional assignments and reward, as the boss thrives on reward for additional assignments.

Movie Stars will absorb very well if there is a full production with lights, cameras and action. They are generally not quick processors, but these learners will absorb more thoroughly by enjoying the full experience of the drama. They absorb more slowly because they're not concerned with the content as much as the boss; they are concerned with the experience; they prefer the scenic route. Without props, audio-visual aids, and humor, you may lose them. They want to be served and academically wined and dined. This group is a bit more moody due to their emotional sensitivity. Teachers should not take mood swings personal, but realize that they are dealing with the kings and queens of drama. As a result, the learning presentation must be dramatic to this group.

Turtles learn best when you slow it down. I mean slow it down significantly. You must keep it simple, slow, and steady. The reason for this slow processing is because these learners are connecting many dots, (well outside the curriculum) and developing a deep understanding from the bottom up. And, when they've got it, they've got it forever. Sometimes, they're mistakenly labeled as learning disabled, especially in light of other quicker learners.

Turtles are not to be devalued because they can make significant contributions on their subject matters. This is true because they're able to internalize deeply and apply wisdom in unique ways. They may be the last to finish reading a passage, but first in understanding. They may also test poorly on exams and standardized tests if they are timed. In an academic environment, turtles are slow methodical processors. Again, they should not be criticized for their slow speed because they have advantages of deeper and more thorough understanding beyond the scope of the content. They will make fewer errors in the long run because they are slow, careful and methodical. They may become frustrated when others move so quickly, especially if they are in error. In addition, I find them to be loyal, sincere, sensitive to criticism and good teacher's pets.

Einstein's will learn well if you explain every detail, explain it well, and answer all of their questions. Unlike turtles who eventually and slowly connect their own dots over time, Einstein's are "aggressively" in pursuit of answers. If you don't have their answers, they will likely find answers themselves before the instructor, as their intellectual appetite will not allow them to rest. The boss wants to quickly complete the task and get done, while the Einstein is in search for more information on the subject, beyond the textbook. They are researchers and seekers of in depth knowledge by nature. Teachers will either love them or … avoid them. To Einstein's, it's all about aggressively getting to the conclusions of tough questions, even if by trial and error. Einstein's live for the challenge. Assignments too easy will send them down a spiral of frustration, disrespect, or perhaps anger. If unengaged, they find their own rabbit trails (things which peaks their interest) and suddenly they're off in outer space - learning what teachers may be unable or unwilling to teach them – due to time, circumstance, or personality mismatch. They may seem to be unruly or disengaged at times, due to confinement. This learning personality could easily be at wits end with their insatiable appetite for more. And, while brilliant, they may appear to be academically subpar, occasionally resulting in behavioral challenges and administrative sanctions. With this group, the instructor must step it up – way up, allow them to pursue their own unique curiosities, while feeding them with the resources they need to develop on their own if necessary. This is an out of the box-learning group. Therefore, keeping them in the box of structure is detrimental to their learning experience, as they thrive on academic freedom.

The Artist is the final major personality group. This personality is fascinated with personally creating something. If they're not creating something in a hands-on environment, they're not terribly excited about learning. You may hear, "I want to try; I want to do it". They're the little cooks in the kitchen; they are the junior mechanics under the hood with dad, in the way of progress - it seems. They must be apart of the instruction and apart of the instructional experience. They don't want to see a demonstration; they want to be the demonstration. They're creative, very creative people. For these learners, body and mind always work in tandem, as it relates to academics. They will always prefer to learn by doing something – anything involving movement and creativity. This group is very innovative because of their inclination to try new and different things or to manipulate the norms. They are naturally funny and upbeat, regardless of the mood of others. They awake vibrant and ready to go. This personality type is plagued by having to sit still or be complacent. If they are not moving and doing something, they are not learning at full throttle.

Note: there are a few caveats to understanding these learning styles. First, a student may possess combinations of learning styles and make transitions from one learning personality to another personality type in different settings and based upon different subjects. Secondly, all students are gifted in a unique area and have a unique skill-set causing them to excel in their area of dominance. When a student is operating in their dominant skill set, the learning dynamics could shift due to their giftedness in that area. Thirdly, there is always an opposite of one's learning personality. These opposite personalities frequently become spouses, friends, or business partners because humanity is attracted to others who are strong in their weaknesses. As a result, students and people (in general) will always marvel someone else, as they are also being marveled based upon their strengths.

Two things will occur as a result of this: 1) Students sometimes acquire the feeling of inferiority because someone else if gifted in their area of weakness. 2) Learners may find themselves fighting with these opposite personalities instead of blending and leveraging their weaknesses.

I submit that it is possible to create a learning environment that draws upon the strengths of each learner. Accent and applaud each child while they are in their strength, so that each student is valued and made to feel special. In addition, I submit that it is possible to allow those who are gifted to the support the instructor in their areas of strength, providing each student has the same opportunity to do so when it comes to their own area of dominance. As a paradigm shift, this cooperative community-style of learning is much more reflective of the world in which we live and is a bit more practical for our multi-dynamic classrooms today.

So, what a job teachers have, right? Actually, what a job parents have because if you're not up to speed on elementary learning styles, your child may be a victim of inadvertent stewardship – no fault to teachers, but circumstance, budgets and politics.

We all must take ownership of our elementary student's learning experience. We must commit to becoming more involved – more involved with learning, working, and playing.

We have the wonderful opportunity to create environments of learning, which will undoubtedly breed unbelievable achievement for an entire lifetime.

LIFE LESSON 6

Master the Middle and High School Stage

I begin by saying, "oh boy". You guessed it. If you think early and elementary learning is a challenge, then middle and high school takes the learning challenge to another level. There is one primary reason. It is because these children are stuck in the middle of childhood and adulthood, while advanced academics are taking place. As the complex process of education is occurring, so is their advanced physical, hormonal, social and emotionally development. Like wild weeds and young trees all growing together in the midst of social pressure, so is the lack of discipline, hormonal imbalances and pop-culture plaguing the minds of young people who inwardly desire to learn.

In order for us to successfully raise the educational bar with our teenagers, we must outwit them and the negative forces upon their educational lives.

It is more difficult for our children today than it was ever before. The social and moral standards are unfortunately challenged and lowered with each generation, even as innovative advancements are also being made; it means that the parental generations are being outwitted with the swift growth of technology and evil temptations of the coming age. It's very tough for our teenagers.

At the middle and high school levels, it's all about strategy. In order for parents to successfully raise the educational bar with our teenagers, we must outwit them and outwit the negative forces upon their educational lives. If we fail to do so, these students will meet stunning consequences, which will cause them to later question our roles in their development.

There are several obstacles, which impact their level of educational success. As a result of these social obstacles, many of our middle and high school students are dropping out of school directly into life, parenthood, drugs, and everything imaginable. The following are a few tips for combating the challenges of teenage academics.

1. <u>You must</u> have a strong defense against negative influences and negative peer pressure, which downplay the emphasis on learning. This must be done daily and by any means necessary.
2. <u>You must</u> take ownership of your student's future and not allow it to be stolen by their mediocrity or lack of understanding. Discuss life goals and ambitions and vigorously work towards them. Until they are 18, you own each decision they make. If necessary, seek counsel and support for important decisions.

3. <u>You must</u> take responsibility for academic performance with a vengeance, so that they won't fall prey to the D averages and the C averages that are often the result of weak academic leadership and stewardship in the home.

It's Time to be the difference. **It's Time** to put it all on the line. You may not have another opportunity to enter this window of change. If you fail to do so, the embedded cycles of mediocrity could frequent their ENTIRE lives for years if not decades to come. Middle and high school academics are very serious business. Not only is it the place where character is built, but it is also the stage where their positions and platforms for life should be defined and solidified before moving on into college or career. If done properly, this will all lead to a very targeted college and career experience.

You have the power to lead them through turbulent waters and to shift their direction for life. Richard Steele (former RNC chairman) once said that true leadership never asks for permission to lead. True leadership in the home is the ability to influence the teenager to follow through inspiration, courage, and the pursuit of great reward. Leadership is also the initiative and responsibility required to own the outcome, whether good or bad. Strong educational leadership is a must for middle and high school students. You must be firm on leading your teenager by example, instead of following your teenager from a position of circumstance or academic inferiority.

Just in case you need permission to lead your child towards the light of a better tomorrow, realize that their Creator gave you two things. You were given the blessing of their birth, and you were given the charge by God to steward their precious life. You are expected to require only the best from your children.

I have made of career in higher education and personal development, as a financial aid director, admissions director, business professor and motivational speaker. I've seen the damage of poor educational stewardship, when it comes to college admissions, scholarship opportunities, college debt, college drop-out, and poor academic achievement overall. Lack of middle and high school focus and discipline are often the culprits. Academic discipline must be perfected at the secondary levels and enforced throughout the latter years.

> *You are expected to require only the best from your children.*

I can't say how important it is for you to become deeply involved in your middle or high school student's academic business.

It literally affects the quality of the rest of their lives, and their children's lives – possibly generations to come. Grades and academic performance are critical to educational success at all levels. If your child is not receiving the academic support they need, then they may be at-risk of facing life-long problems that statistically follow children who perform poorly in school.

You must pinpoint any hindrances to high academic performance by first asking yourself if you're the first hindrance. Are you personally providing the additional daily support that your teenager needs? Then ask yourself if the domestic environment you've created is a hindrance in any way. Examine your schedule and social life to determine if it allows you to support your student properly. Then, examine your student's friends and social networks for hindrances. After which, make some decisions.

As a young child, I was in a gifted learning group in school - around 3rd and 4th grade. I was informed that I was reading on a college level in 5th grade. However, by the time I entered my senior year of high school, I had nearly flunked out of high school; I had extremely poor SAT scores and a terrible military aptitude test – or ASVAB. I was on my way to enlistment in Uncle Sam's Army in a low-grade army job. I was as confused about life and education as anyone else I could think of. Still somehow being offered a scholarship for college on musical talent, I chose the military because I wanted to support my family as quickly as possible. However, that was not my responsibility and I did not have the personal discipline nor the academic strength to detach myself from where I was headed.

After a short and difficult stint in the military, bankruptcy, foreclosure, and 10 additional years of life headed nowhere, I realized that I still did not like the direction that I was headed in life. With God's help and the help of a mentor, Dr. Lonnie Sessoms, I decided to turn a corner towards the direction of education – my innate strength from a child. After 5 short years, I took another look at myself. I had a bachelor of science with a double major, two master degrees, and had begun working on my doctorate. Rock bottom is unfortunately the greatest place to be for a life change. Had I the educational leadership required early on, I would have avoided rock bottom and a 20-year delay to my place of peace.

Yet, I suddenly realized that it was not how I started, but it was how I chose to end my educational pursuit. Don't accept current educational challenges as the end of the road for your teenager, during middle and high school. Never give up on destiny; as soon as you make the decision to be the difference, you can turn your educational positioning around at any stage of life.

> *Don't accept current educational challenges as the end of the road for you or your teenager.*

Imagine if I had ended my educational career with my failure of high school – never to sit in another classroom again. As a result, I would have never taught in a collegiate classroom later on. High school would have been the end of the road for me. It was all avoidable.

Imagine if I had not gone through a family divorce at age 12, or if I had not gone through a dozen schools in seemingly a half dozen years. What if I had been tutored while in school? Would I have taken the same path of life or had the same outcome? Imagine if I had been placed in a college-prep program, or if I had been enrolled in a SAT or ASVAB workshop. Imagine if educational excellence was demanded of me daily. Imagine if there was a college fund set aside to assist me with the insurmountable debt I had incurred. Would my experience have been different with different levels of support? This is not only my story; it is our story. It is your story in some variation and the story of so many children dealing with significant issues of life and learning.

You will hear this story again later in life, if you don't take action. It's Time. Please do not ignore this call to resolve your place of peace in the educational lives of your children – our children. Every family in America is dealing with some form of struggle. Yet, no one has an excuse to retreat to mediocrity, when it involves the development of our children and teenagers. The results are too devastating. Fight for life. Fight for success in education.

I am reminded of President Obama's mother who, in the face of employment, international travel, civil rights controversy, mixed marriage challenges, divorce, sickness, and single-parenthood, embraced the call to raise a president. Did she know she was training a president? No, she was simply committed to her call, as a parent. She found a way to ensure that her student received the best educational foundation despite the school, challenges, or the circumstances. To the extent that she would rise early in the morning to ensure that she had time to tutor her student before work, she would unknowingly tutor a future president.

This academic discipline and commitment to excellence apparently instilled fundamental study ethics, which Mr. Obama would later draw upon. Early foundations allowed him to later accomplish unbelievable academic success, which included being voted in as the first African-American president of the Harvard Law School Review. The fundamental disciplines demanded by a single parent would later stem a string of first accomplishments by this student. Awards and accomplishments, such as the Noble Peace Prize are possible to those who choose to make the tough choices early.

This is the difference that educational emphasis can make early on. As you can see, high school is not the perfect place to fix an academic problem; academic habits should be well established in the early years. However, middle and high school are where those academic habits are perfected and protected from intruders, as academic success can erode with the waves of life and the seas of excessive change.

At middle and high school, our students are either academic performers or they are academic victims of circumstance. Nevertheless, wherever you are, the game is not over until you win.

LIFE LESSON 7
Master the Collegiate Stage

C ollege at the undergraduate level can be wonderfully scary. There's money involved, students are moving away, there are the unknown professors, and there is the hidden party animal in most students, which every student wants to disguise and deny. College is where the high school caterpillar becomes a butterfly, and begins the unstable flight towards independence and exploration.

The traditional eighteen year-old or the older adult college student will have many college hoops through which to jump – the hoop of admissions, the hoop of funding, the hoop of independence, then the hoop of academic performance. It is important to be well informed on all facets of the college experience in order to provide adequate support for your college student.

Admissions

Admission to college is not very difficult, especially if you're looking to enter one of the lower tiered schools or community colleges. Mostly every school is ranked in terms of student body size, prestige, endowed funds, admissions criteria, and often, academic rigor. Schools are ranked in tiers one (I) through four (IV). Although rankings change frequently, a tier-one school may be Harvard, Duke, UNC-Chapel Hill, or Howard. A tier-two school may be Florida State, Colorado State, or Washington State. A tier-three school may be Hofstra, Old Dominion, George Mason, etc. And, a tier-four school may be Clark Atlanta, East Carolina, Florida A&M, Georgia State, Tennessee State, and North Carolina A&T. These rankings all depend upon the latest listings of the U.S. News & World Report College Rankings. My listings here should not be taken as the latest or most accurate. This is for example.

At any rate, your student's academic preparation will naturally place them into one of these four tiers. You should know which tier you are on and be prepared to adjust your tier-track if desired.

As you probably know, one of the biggest contributors to college admissions is past test scores and historical academic performance from high school. For admissions into one of the higher tiered schools, the GPA needs to be in the 3.5 range and above. For admissions into some of the lowered tiered schools, a GPA in the range of 3.0 would be acceptable. For admissions into a junior college or a forgiving tier-four school, a GPA of between 2.0 to 3.0 may be acceptable, depending upon the school.

Entrance exams are to some schools the most important admissions factor, although many schools will not admit that. SAT scores or ACT scores are absolutely critical to initial admission into an upper-tiered school. My suggestion is to prepare, prepare, and prepare. Believe it or not, there is always a science to scoring well on entrance exams. Although, I am certainly not a scientist in that area, scientists are available for your support. Getting the hang of standardized testing can be expensive, sometimes it's well worth the money to purchase a testing guide or high-end workshop from the professionals, who have superior understanding of entrance exams. In fact, those who create these exams also train the test takers for a fee. You might seek out the creators of the exam and pursue their training workshops before settling on a poor test score.

College Transfer

If increasing test scores is too problematic, costly or intimidating for you, I have a little secret for gaining admissions to practically any college in the world, regardless of rank, tier level or cost. It's called college transfer. It's one of the most hidden secrets to high-end college entrance. You can have the lowest SAT scores in the world, the lowest high school GPA in the world, but if you've been admitted to practically any four-year school and maintained an excellent GPA, you can usually transfer to practically any other four-year school. This does not apply in every case, but 80% of top-tier schools will accept a good performing transfer.

In college transfer admissions, higher-tiered schools no longer regard high school performance or admissions test scores, they're primarily interested in current GPA and current college performance. To get more information, don't take my word for it, call any university and ask about their transfer criteria. I think you'd be amazed.

The problem with most students transferring from one school to another is that they simply don't want to transfer once they get settled. Students get settled with a few friends, they get used to the school, they get used to the college lifestyle and sometimes poor study habits, which are not tolerated at top-tier schools. As a result, they lose sight on the possibility to upgrading to a higher-end school, which could add tens of thousands of dollars to their initial salary offer upon graduation.

The truth is; future employment and graduate admissions are often more about the name of your graduating institution. Few schools will admit this, but as a higher education professional, I know it's true. A low GPA bachelor's from Harvard is still going to open more doors than a very high GPA from a non-ranked Internet school. You only have one chance to transfer and it's at the undergraduate level and before you acquire x amount of credits. You will not normally be able to transfer successfully at the graduate level.

One last tip on the subject – Do not attempt to transfer to an academically rigorous school, if you don't plan to buckle down and perform. You will only flunk out. Make sure that before you transfer, you're ready for college, sleepless nights, the writing lab, everyday tutoring, and a lifestyle of study versus party. If you're ready, you can excel in life and academics by quickly getting your footing with a bachelor's from an upper tiered college or university. This will undoubtedly place you in the running for better graduate school admissions and better career placement.

Financial Aid

Financial aid is one of the most important offices on campus, as it relates to receiving accommodations and paid tuition. Understanding financial aid can save lots of time and money. This section will provide a brief overview of financial aid and how it can help or hurt you. There are traditionally 4 types of financial aid - grants, scholarships, work study and loans. The FAFSA is the beginning point to receiving all college financial aid.

The FAFSA

The FAFSA (pronounced faf-sah) stands for Free Application (for) Federal Student Aid. Basically, this is a federal application, which pre-qualifies you or your student for financial aid of almost any kind. Any student in America who is getting a federal student loan, federal grant, state grant, or work-study placement must apply for financial aid using this online (government) application called the FAFSA. To complete the application, you will need two items. You will need your (your families) tax returns for the previous year and the ability to answer basic financial questions about your household's history, make-up, taxes, and income. Secondly, you will need a federal pin number, which will allow you to electronically sign your application when completed.

> *....if you're considering financial aid, start early – at least a year in advance – minimum.*

You can receive all of this information from the federal FAFSA website. This government website will never be a dot com site. Be aware of sites seeking to assist you for a fee. The official site is fafsa.ed.gov. Please keep in mind that the FAFSA Application and the Federal Pin Number are both free of charge.

Finally, if you're considering financial aid, start early – at least a year in advance - minimum. If your family is in the middle income or upper income brackets, you need to start saving two decades in advance, in order to avoid the stiff loans and the disaster of delivering your student to their college campus with no money. Yes, it can be embarrassing if you are in the upper income brackets with no financial plans. I've seen many pitiful faces in shock of reality sitting across from my desk, as a financial aid director. Prepare as soon as you learn of the expenses you face. Starting early is your best defense.

Financial aid offices are usually helpful, but sometimes, depending upon the school, these offices can leave you totally exposed to your own financial ignorance. Don't always expect hand-holding from the professionals. Occasionally, you'll find an office that won't accept phone calls, emails, and surprisingly, walk-ins. It can be tough; so parents, do your homework years in advance.

Grants

A grant is free money that can be used for college tuition and expenses. You neither have to work for a grant nor repay it. There are several types of federal, state, public, and private grants. But, the most common grant is the Federal Pell Grant.

The Federal Pell Grant is an entitlement that any good-standing American citizen will receive, providing they meet basic institutional and federal requirements. To receive the Pell Grant, the household income cannot exceed middle class income, which begins at approximately $40,000. There are special cases, when family's can have their income adjusted or lowered to receive the Pell Grant. This Grant historically provides support between $5,000 and $6,000 per academic year. For an inexpensive lower-tiered state school, the Pell Grant may be enough to pay tuition. However, for a top tiered school, this will not be enough funding, forcing students into debt before they have a job to pay for it. My advice is to begin making phone calls. Develop a strategy that will help you fund all expenses well before college years. Or, you may frugally accept low-interest federal loans, if you qualify – 95% of applicants qualify.

Need-Based Grants

The federal government determines if the Pell Grant will be awarded as full percentage or partial percentage by generating an EFC – Expected Family Contribution. This is a computer generated code provided by the U.S. Department of Education. This EFC code determines if your family has financial need. It also determines the degree of need, based upon your social and tax information. Depending upon the degree of financial need, indicated by the EFC, your financial aid advisor will make a determination if there are need based grants available to you. The Pell Grant is one such grant. There are dozens of need based grants that can be obtained through a visit to your financial aid office or through a database search of "need-based grants".

Merit-Based Grants

If there is little financial need in the household, then merit-based grants will be one of several remaining choices for funding college. Merit-based grants are programs which offer funding based upon high academic performance, agreement to study in a certain field, or affiliation with a certain organization offering funding for those with high academic promise. There are many opportunities available to those who are willing to make phone calls and do research. Once again, as a former financial aid director, I would begin strategizing the college funding game well in advance – 20, 15, 10 years in advance. You can never begin looking for college funding too early. If you neglect to do so, there will be plenty of interest thirsty loan originators waiting to plague your future with the same number of years of your neglect - 10, 15, even 20 years of student loan repayment. Do the research as soon as possible and begin preparing.

Scholarships

When many think of the word scholarship, for some reason the thought of a full ride from the university enters the mind. A scholarship is any amount of free money that a student can apply to college tuition and expenses. In essence, five dollars can be a scholarship. One dollar, one thousand or ten thousand dollars can be a scholarship. A good outlook on scholarships is this - any amount is appreciated and the more the merrier.

As a financial aid professional, I once applied 6 different scholarships to a student's account, all of which the student solicited on her own. While other students were getting a full ride on need-based funding, this one particular student (whose parents made a nice income, but did not save) funded her entire tuition and fees, simply by asking her parent's employers, her church, the neighborhood cleaners, her family's associations, the utility company, and everyone else she could think of who might have been able to help her.

It was absolutely one of the most fascinating things I had ever seen. Although I had told many students to seek out these funds, this young lady literally did what I was suggesting and paid for her own tuition and expenses, without the financial support of her parents, government assistance or student loans. In some cases, she had to write a letter; in other cases, I had to communicate with various donors on her behalf to validate her requests. Occasionally, I needed to write a letter for her. But, in the end, she found her own funding.

Surprisingly, most of her sponsors did not require some high GPA or extraordinary skill to acquire the scholarship. In fact, some companies didn't have such a scholarship fund, but they made one for this young lady who requested support. I was surprised with how many companies were willing to help someone who wasn't afraid to ask for help. This is the beauty of scholarships. Most of the time, you are required to earn scholarships through athletics or academics. Other times, you are awarded funding simply for asking.

Work Study

Work-study is a federal program, which allows students to earn an income that can either be applied to college tuition and expenses or to personal and academic needs while in college. Work-study is also based on the FAFSA and the EFC. In other words, it has a bit to do with financial need as well. When filling out the FAFSA, you will have the opportunity to indicate whether you're interested in work-study.

Work-study is a great way to subside the use of loans and personal savings. However, it is employment, which can pull the student away from study if you're not careful. Work-study may also be an opportunity to gain an away-from-home support system and a stronger connection with the institution. I generally recommend it. As work-study positions are first-come first-serve, these limited positions can be quickly depleted. If interested, take my advice and inquire early with a department in your area of study.

Loans

There are two major types of loans, private loans and government-based loans. Private loans have absolutely nothing to do with the FAFSA process. Private loans are based upon credit and collateral, just as any other private loan. On the other hand, government based loans are determined through the FAFSA process. The government "will" loan you money providing you or your parents have little to no financial resources. Of course, this is providing you or your parents are not in bankruptcy or in default in another government backed student loan.

> *I absolutely DO NOT recommend student loans*
> ....

Private loans and government loans are risky business. It's risky because they are easy to acquire, and very difficult to eliminate. A student loan can take you on the ride of your life. The compound interest, the affects upon your credit, and the affects upon your household income can be nothing short of an absolute nightmare.

I absolutely DO NOT recommend student loans, unless you have absolutely no choice. And then, I still am reluctant to recommend student loans because there is always another choice though perhaps difficult to discover. You have the choice of waiting. Wait and save. Or, if you have no money, wait and seek scholarships. Waiting is an option; the military college programs are options. For example, consider ROTC, which can pay all of one's college expenses. Consider loan forgiveness programs for teaching or working in a government or social

> *There are many creative ways to pay for college, if you will step outside of the status quo of others and strategically ponder ways around the high costs of tuition.*

services capacity. Consider the many scholarship opportunities out there for those who ask. Consider paying out of pocket installments to a nearby university; live with relatives to avoid dorm expenses; pay for a few classes per year versus heavy loads that you cannot afford. As my father would always say, you probably have more time than money, so spend time and save money.

There are many creative ways to pay for college, if you will step outside of the status quo of others and strategically ponder ways around the high costs of tuition. There is always employment or the tuition reimbursement programs through employers with those benefits. Many employers will pay you to finish school. In short, there is funding out there for those who plan, plan well, and plan in advance. Be very cautious about loans.

In fact, I'll share my story. When I walked out of graduate school with a bachelor and two master degrees, I owed nearly $100,000 in student loan debt, and had a $1,200 per month loan payment awaiting me. No one explained the depth of the future awaiting me. I'm coaching you from the high price of experience. No one gave me the information that I'm giving you. I did not know about college transfer. For that kind of money, I should have had degrees from Yale and Oxford. Take it from me, ignorance is expensive. So, do me a favor; do your children a favor; Heed. Take my knowledge and my life experiences and become more successful, a lot faster.

College Life

I have a very short philosophy about college life. College life can be the rest of your life. If you don't live college life as if it were the rest of your life, you will soon have no life at all. In nearly a decade of higher education experience, I have seen immaturity devastate athletic dreams, employment dreams, and financial dreams. On the other hand, I have seen students in college, who had absolutely no business in college whatsoever. College is not some mandatory experience for a great life.

I was nearly thirty before I returned to college, after dropping out with a 1.4 GPA. However, when I returned, as a married man, who had experienced the brutalities of life, I knew college was serious business and I knew it would affect the rest of my life. Sometimes, the best decision for a youth is to wait a bit, before attending college. Every student will simply not have the motivation, the academic fortitude, or the disciplined life skills necessary to succeed in college - at least not so quickly after high school graduation. Many students are ready. Others are not. I was not ready.

After high school, I almost immediately enlisted with the U.S. Army. After the first few weeks, I knew right away that military life wasn't for me either. My drill sergeants would tell me that after basic training, I would enjoy the real army. But, I had problems with the discipline before the military, during the military, and after the military. I wasn't prepared for military life either. Upon my miraculous honorable discharge from military service, I eagerly entered the college experience. But, guess what? I flunked out after about a year. Still, I wasn't ready. It took another 8 years before I would be ready for the discipline of college academics.

As an older adult in class with students much younger than I, I could look across the classroom and identify my younger self in other students. I knew they weren't ready. I could also look across the classroom and identity my older self. You see, what I saw in the same college classroom were teenagers, young parents, middle-agers, and senior citizens. You would be surprised of the amount of 50+ and 60+ students sitting in college seats. I quickly realized that successful college life depended upon maturity and academic readiness, not age. The pitfall is that we often turn the word "wait" into "never". Don't give up on academics.

If one is not ready for college life, take my recommendation. Wait. A 2.0 undergrad degree or a 2.5 undergrad degree is very often no good for future endeavors. As a graduate admissions officer, I would be forced to ask a 40 year-old successful teacher, why they once had a 2.5 undergraduate GPA years earlier and are now looking to enter a masters degree program. All the while I knew the answer. The truth is, your academic history will always follow you. Ask President George W. Bush. One can take lemons and make good lemonade, but it may take a world of sugar to remove the tangy taste, even many years later.

As an older adult, my ending GPA on my bachelor of science was a 3.67. It would have been much higher had the 1.4 GPA from 10 years prior not been factored in. Otherwise, I would have graduated summa cum laude. In other words, because of history and the past academic performance of a young man not quite ready for college life, I had to continue to drink my own bitter lemonade many years later. I was still very excited to graduate, but I also realized that life plays for keeps. On a good note, I was inducted into an adult academic honor society for being in the top 10% of my class; I got into graduate school and went onto to begin doctoral level study. If you're a turtle like me, never count yourself out. It's not too late. The favorite book says, "The race is not given to the swift or the strong, but to the one who endures".

How To Make A's In College

It took me a while to acquire the following academic secrets, but I finally secured them after a bit of determination. Just to give you a little confidence in my techniques, I went back through my undergraduate and graduate transcripts and counted 38 accredited college courses where I received an A+, A, or A-. That's well over 100 credit hours of A-level college credit. This is not to boast, but to give you a little confidence that I fully understand how to be successful in the classroom.

The A+ Personality

"A" students are simply "A" students – not by birth, but by decision. Once you mentally become an "A" student, not only do you expect to make an "A" in every course, but everyone else, including the instructor expects you to make an "A". The "A" becomes your identifiable personality.

As an adjunct business professor in the classroom for four years, I could spot an "A" student, from their introduction – "hello". They are the first in everything. They submit their assignments first, they get to class first; they often sit on the first row; they're the first to volunteer; they take the first responsibilities in group projects; they're the first to ask questions; they're the first to complete the reading assignments; they have become first people – "A" people.

Let me be clear. This is learned behavior. Anyone can be an "A" student, but there is a price. You must forsake everything else for first place – the "A" place. You'll need to forsake the night socials, sometimes evening programs, the dance at the club, the romantic date, the shopping excursion, and sometimes the "everyone's-going" trip to the amusement park. Why? Because, to an "A" student, the "A" comes first. It's all about first things first to an "A" student.

I remember, as an "A" student feeling VERY disappointed if I did not get an "A" for a class. For the most part, "A" students feel the same way. We make it known to the instructor, students, and everyone else that we're looking for an "A" out of the course.

The "A" personality is a battle-ready frame of mind. You, the student, are battling against anything that stands in your way. You readily battle against being unprepared by preparing well in advance. You battle against tests, by discovering as much about your tests as possible. You sit with the professor in private meetings; you take notes and clues about each assignment and prepare vigorously. When it comes to the classroom, the "A" student always has that "battle-ready" "show-time" face. It's a frame of mind. Simply put, we're ready. Always.

Speed Reading

Speed reading is a technique that I learned while in undergrad. I actually learned to speed read through a university-sponsored workshop. Being a turtle, I was very slow in my reading. I mean very slow. I would focus on every word, one line at a time. I was so slow and detailed in my reading that I sometimes lost the overall gist. I had a problem and I wasn't sure how to fix it. I actually thought something was wrong with me. I was so slow that I would mentally drift off into daydreaming while reading. Though my eyes were locked on the words, my mind was often miles elsewhere. When I say slow, I mean slooowwww.

Speed reading is not a part of the grammar school curriculum. No one told me that I could read two hundred words per minutes, which is much faster than my rate of speech. I later learned that I was reading too slowly to stimulate my brain and keep my own interest. Think about it. Speech too slow is painful and speech too fast is frustrating. There is a listening speed that is perfect for you. Likewise, there is a reading speed that is perfect for your brain. And, it's considerably faster than you were traditionally trained to read and even speak. Learn to read much faster. Your brain can handle more than you realize.

Here's what I learned in this speed reading class years ago. Your brain and eyes can actually absorb words on a page exponentially faster than you can speak or even listen – even as fast as 800 words per minute for some. In fact, the only hindrance your brain has in absorbing words on a page is your ability to lay your eyes upon the words. In essence, as fast as you can see the words, you can read the words. That's much faster than you can formulate silent speech in your mind.

We often confuse reading with mental speech. Speed reading and mental reading are two totally different processes at two different rates of speed. Speed reading is the mental absorption of written words seen in any direction. It is not pondering every single word or the even silent pronunciation of the words in your mind. Silent pronunciation dramatically slows your reading speed. However, you'll need to find your own comfortable pace, which is faster than you can mentally enunciate, but yet comfortable enough for you to comprehend.

Speed reading requires trusting your mind to grasp what you cannot articulate. Honestly, it feels like massive skimming and not reading at all. However, if your eyes have made contact with the words and you're absorbing in a quiet and focused state of mind, you can "absorb" an entire book (an easy read) in a couple hours. You may not be able to pass a test on it the first time around, but you'll gradually learn to consume larger amounts of text much more efficiently with practice.

When preparing for a complicated exam, there will be occasions when you'll need to stop and ponder, let's say mathematical equations or complicated concepts. However, many college texts are easy reads, which will allow you to effectively and efficiently gain the concepts of the book without spending hours and hours reading.

Speed reading requires practice. The more you practice, the better you will read. If you want to give it a try, here's what I recommend. Make three quick passes of a chapter or book. The first pass, look only at the table of contents or the headings, as you flip through the book. The next pass, look at the words in bold, all words in italics, and any exhibits or pictures. After you've built a framework for which to absorb the material, do the following. Use the pointer finger and middle finger of the same hand and make a third pass over each line of the written text as fast as your eyes can move. Don't formulate words in your mind; just move your eyes over the words as quickly as possible. Go over a page and then stop to ponder your comprehension. In other words, determine if you actually understood what you saw. Practice moving your eyes over the words faster and faster on each page – much faster than you can speak.

What you will find over time and over a few months of practice is that you'll be able to do three things.

a. You'll be able to retain enough information about the subject matter that will allow you to speak on the subject.

b. You'll be able to construct mental landmarks about where certain information is located in the reading, in the event you need to return to read a portion of the text more carefully.

c. And, you'll be able to cover much more literary ground and get more done by using this technique – not to mention that it makes the academic experience more enjoyable and less boring.

Overall, you'll gain an edge – a big edge over your peers and your own challenges to learn and to do well in academics using speed reading.

The Highlighter & The Pen

As simple as it sounds, a highlighter makes a significant difference in retention. Use a highlighter to refresh your memory of important items in the text. Use the pen; write in the book. On a college level, when you purchase your books, you may write in the book; many students refrain from doing so, looking to sell the books back to the bookstore. Use any tool necessary to assist you with recalling certain information. Your understanding derived from writing in the book may be worth more than the bookstore reimbursement in the end.

Much of your college success will require you to recall blocks of information. Make a little song, a little rhyme, a mental picture of the blocks of information that you'll need to recall. These little techniques can become your personal answer keys which will assist you with recall. With your pen, take notes, draw images about the lectures. This will quadruple your chances of recall.

While in undergrad, I took a music appreciation course. In the course, students were required to recall the names of the classical composition, even though the music had no lyrics. Here's what I did. Mentally, I added my own lyrics to the song. I learned to sing the actual title of the song (which had not lyrics) as the music played, thereby strategically highlighting the music with my own answers – all for the exam. Today, when I hear certain pieces of classical music, while strolling through the mall, I'm amazed that I can still identify the titles and composers because of my added lyrics. You can do the same things with other subjects using mental pictures and verbal connections, acronyms that you create, and other mental highlights. Make notes and get creative with the pen. You can actually make learning a lot of fun.

Anyone can teach you subject matter, but few will teach you how to learn. I strongly suggest developing ways and means of absorbing and recalling material – this is learning. To do so means higher GPAs, higher test scores, and higher academic ambitions for life-long learners.

Get to know Your Professor

Every professor has preferences. No two professors are exactly alike. Studying the preferences of each professor is very important. Your grades often depend upon how well you follow their instructions. Sometimes, the instructions are incredibly simple, but the penalties for not heeding these simple instructions can be very costly.

Get to know your professors by carefully reading the syllabus, listening carefully when they speak, and asking lots of questions. Professors usually welcome questions, even if they are simple questions. Being intellectuals, instructors love to answer questions and solve problems, even if the problems and questions are minor. They get a kick out of it. So, don't be afraid to ask questions, this is one of the few ways to know what they're thinking.

Professors usually have office hours. Make a visit, especially when there's something you don't understand. Always remember that the professor works for you. And, they generally want to spend time with those who want to learn. In addition, the best way to get a little grace and forgiveness during a time when you haven't fully grasped key concepts is by having built an academic relationship with your professor. Sometimes, it makes all the difference in the world during grading. Moreover, professors make great recommenders. Good recommendations come from those with whom you've built strong academic relations.

Get Involved / Be Aware

Know what's going on around campus. Participate in productive extra-curricular activities. Be sure that these activities don't interrupt important studies, but be aware of key events and activities, which will be able to aid you in gaining a deeper understanding of school and life.

A College Diet

The major contributors to brainpower are diet and exercise. You are what you eat. You can do what you prepare your mind and body to do. Eating junk food and foods high in fat, sodium, and sugar will put your brain on a mental strike. You will be out to lunch the entire day, if you fail to ingest the proper diet for learning.

Your brain is comprised of mostly water. To prepare for heavy mental processing, you need to be dedicated to drinking water – lots of it. Water allows you to properly hydrate your system. Exercise allows you to properly flush your body of impurities and mental sludge, which unclog your faculties. In addition, water is a good conduit for electricity. Brain impulses are nothing more than weak electricity, which flow through the brain which is 70% water. High fat content, such as cheese and fried foods are not good conduits, but foods high in water content and complex carbohydrates or natural sugars are much better.

Aside from plenty of rest, healthy eating is the most important thing you can do to physically prepare yourself for college study. The best diet for study and intense dialogue is a diet high in fruits and veggies. A diet low in concentrated protein and low in simple carbohydrates is a good diet for study. In contrast, once again, what you need are complex carbohydrates, water and plenty of natural sugars.

Your brain and body gets a tremendous boost from natural sugars. However, from simple sugars found in snacks and candy, your body gets a tremendous downward spike in energy, which makes you sleepy and drowsy after the sugar rush is over. I can easily identify those in class who had walked over to class while eating a belly full of candy and chips. They will appear to be totally wiped out by the quick drop in energy, resulting from high sugar content in their system. Bad student, right? No, just a poor study diet.

> *Aside from plenty of rest, healthy eating is the most important thing you can do to physically prepare for college study.*

Eating complex carbohydrates such as potatoes, brown rice and oats will prevent an energy drop and allow a long and consistent flow of energy, as your body takes longer to digest these complex carbs. However, do not eat heavy amounts of anything. Eat very light protein (meats, greasy foods, etc, peanut butter & cheese). Carry natural fruits and veggies to eat as needed in class. Examples would be raisins, grapes, carrots, apples, bananas, pears, and oranges, etc. Due to extremely high sugar content, beware of fruit juices, even 100% juices. The term "from concentrate" generally means high in sugar – even natural sugar. Practicing these techniques will prepare you to succeed in college.

Master Key 2
Raise The Bar For Career Development

Everyone has a calling or a purpose in life, as we discussed. It's wonderful when one's calling and career are the same. In fact, through my research and life lessons learned, it should be this way. I believe that with focus and great determination you can make your calling your career. This stage of utopia, where your hobby or passion becomes your career, comes at different stages on the timeline of life. Some unify their career and calling or passion as children, while others find themselves completing many years of school. Yet others enter this stage after they have experienced a significant portion of life. Some began singing as children and have developed lucrative careers from singing; for others, sports, or writing, or drawing, or organizing have been their passion. Whatever it is, make your love your life. You'll never find a competitor who can do what you do - your way – better than you. When you've found what you love to do, you will do it for free, as the pay is an extra bonus.

> *Make your love your life.*

> *You'll never find a competitor who can do what you do – your way – better than you.*

You should know your path and own it for life. Refrain from changing careers, until you identify your love and your passion. Once your find it, stay on course for life. Only you can successfully live your life. So, make it a good one and most of all, enjoy it. As my friend and mentor Les Brown says, "stop making a living and begin living your making". **It's Time to actively develop a passionate career.**

There is one additional key to enjoying your passion or hobby as the primary source of your income. It is the age old principle of supply and demand. Whether you are offering a service or a product, there must be demand for your career or your business. If there is little to no demand for what you do then, there is going to be little to no income generated, right? Wrong.

As an adjunct business professor, I know that you can alter or create demand. In other words, people will buy mostly any product or service, if you can meet their expectations and present what you have in such a way that they say YES. Yes, I will buy; or yes, you are hired.

Five Keys For Getting To Yes.

1. **Love** what you do and love yourself. Customers first feed from your personal confidence and excitement.

2. **Know** your product, service, or skill better than anyone else. You must be the expert on your career or business. Study it, learn it, so that you can safely say, I'm an expert on..._____ You can be from Mars, but if you're the real expert, you will be hired and your product will be sold.

3. **Invest** money into packaging yourself, your skill and your product. Though you may be an expert, you must package yourself as an expert. Get the certificate, get the degree, get the professional equipment, hire the marketing professional, get the franchise, purchase the new suit or uniform, and package yourself. Invest in you, and others will be inclined to also invest in you.

4. **Identify** the people who love what you do. Since you have the supply, look for the demand. Look for a place where your potential customers (your market) are in large quantities, and place yourself in the middle of your market.

5. **Sell**. If you're looking for a job, you must sell yourself. If you're looking to exchange a product or service for compensation, you must sell it. In other words, learn how to sell. Selling is a science and an art. Selling is the last step. And, if you've mastered steps 1 through 4, selling is a much easier process.

My Definition for selling: Being able to express the full value and benefit of your monetized item, in such a way that the potential buyer understands how they would advance themselves from the purchase of your product.

Why The Sun Shines

A Career is like a tower of security, until stock markets crash,
Always answering chores and tasks simply for a little more cash.

Isn't cash the name of the game?, or so it is we're told,
But, the real beauty of my divinely chosen career is that it never gets old.

Why do we labor with our hands, our feet, and our minds?
Because labor is a joy when it's my divinely chosen career;
It is why the sun shines.

– Joe McDaniel

LIFE LESSON 8
10 Keys To Developing Your Career

1. Determine Your Career

One of the most important tasks in career development is pinpointing your profession. Not only is it important that others clearly understand your profession, but you need to clearly understand your profession.

In short, everyone should be able to verbalize his or her profession or career in one word. A profession may end with one of the following suffixes: er, or, ant, etc. For example, one may identify himself or herself as a laborer, banker, pastor, professor, teacher, painter, author, driver or accountant. Of course, there are exceptions to this rule of thumb. For example, professions such as the clerk, a mechanic, artist, or police will not have such suffixes. In any event, the one word identification is necessary in order to properly develop your career. Ask yourself, what is my life-long career or calling in one word?

In hopes of gaining employment, many will routinely accept any position that comes their way. Be cautious of changing careers too frequently. Changing employers is much less harmful than changing careers. A single career enables one to amass experience over the course of many years. This experience adds considerable value to the development of your career and income potential. The idea is to discover a career, which suits your interests, values, and life goals. Once you have identified the career that is perfect for you, commit to it for a lifetime of at least 20 years.

Carefully consider your desired profession? If you have difficulty determining your profession, you might solicit professional consultation to help determine the right profession for you.

2. Credentials/Certifications

Once your career has been well determined, it is usually necessary to obtain necessary training in order to effectively operate in your profession. Depending upon its nature, necessary training could include formal education or informal education. Formal education generally denotes a classroom format, which results in some sort of diploma or certificate. Informal training can be obtained on an employment site or through self-training.

The career itself often determines the type of training that is necessary. Many professions are regulated to ensure professional standards. For example, becoming a certified public accountant (CPA) requires a baccalaureate degree and a satisfactory score on a standardized exam. Becoming a general contractor also requires the study of building regulations and an exam, which results in a license to practice building. Cosmetology, trucking, law enforcement, and even business ownership are all careers, which require some form of preparation and licensing.

Credentials are a way of modern life. These are man-made barriers for the good of the public. Though challenging at times, don't view the credentialing process as an impossible challenge to overcome. Welcome the challenge and master it. You'll be glad you did.

3. Continuing Education Credit

Likewise, once you've securely established your career, you must continue to develop. Few things stay the same. As things change and as new knowledge is created, each of us must be updated with changing information.

It is vitally important to attend conferences, seminars, courses and other training to continue the advancement process. Learning can never be excluded from growth. In fact, growing is learning. Growth is development. In other words, you will grow to the extent that you are willing to learn. If for some reason you are not developing or advancing in your career, it is likely because you have stopped learning. *To get more, you must know more.*

Ever heard of the term R&D or Research and Development? Every successful manufacturing company has an R&D division. Research is a part of the learning process. Research enables you to either create new knowledge or discover new knowledge. A growing career is a learning career. Engage in personal research and development.

4. Association Membership

Another vehicle of learning is being connected with those who are more knowledgeable in your field. Rubbing shoulders with those who've been where you're going is important. It's an easier way to learn.

Consider membership with a professional association in your field. Occasionally, you may find yourself a bit reluctant to connect with others who may appear to be your competitors, but take a different perspective. Associations are for the betterment of the field at large. There is a substantial amount of power in numbers. Only those who really care about the industry want to see it grow and develop.

In professional associations, you'll find that members make positive trade-offs, which make membership worthwhile. You may have developed a technique or philosophy that saves money, while another colleague may have developed a technique that saves time. When you come together to share ideas, you can collaborate on both saving time and money.

There is much value in joining an association. Speaking of value, there is usually an investment required. Please don't allow the investment fee of the membership to deter you. Anything worth having is worth the investment.

5. Books & Articles

Books and field-based writings are the oldest form of training and education. It is absolutely vital that you read, read, and read. Often the success or failure you experience can be traced back to your reading and personal development or lack thereof, respectively. Needless to say, if you aren't reading, you're likely not experiencing the successes you desire.

A book could contain as much as 20-40 years of someone's experience and good advice – all in two inches of bound paper. Talking about value, who would not want the experience of someone's entire life or career in exchange for 15 or 20 dollars? Books will enable you to reduce painful problems. A book is usually well worth the small price.

The beauty of reading is that it allows you to eliminate years of struggle and confusion from your career. One of the most productive things that you can do to accelerate your career is to seek out and a good book each month. I may purchase a dozen books in one visit to the book store.

However, there is one caveat to acquiring knowledge through books. You must actually read what you've purchased. As silly as it sounds, the book will do you no good collecting dust on the shelf. Set a discipline to at least thumb through a book weekly. If you're not an avid reader, then look for something that catches your eye, as you flip through the pages. Crack the book.

I have hundreds of books. I have not read them all. Absolutely not. However, the stimulating charge from the knowledge of hundreds of experts in my library builds incredible confidence. When I need a boost on a subject or when I'm having trouble in a certain area, I go to my library. I believe that I have the answer to nearly any challenge I'm facing on my book shelve. The fact is, I know where to go when I need help. Invest in your career by building a reservoir of knowledge and experience to draw from for years to come. Read

6. Business Cards/Brochures

Absolutely no one should be in a career without a business card. Keep in mind, careers are for life; so then, business cards are for life. Your business card should be like a union card to remind you and others of the contributions that you are making to society.

Don't see your career as a means to paying bills. See your career as a means to impact the world. You are a servant looking for an opportunity to inspire someone, help someone, and change the course of history for the better. You are able to accomplish this through your God-given gifts, your abilities - your career. Remember from the introduction, your gifts are an indication of what areas you are called to support.

Never be afraid to publish who you are, not necessarily whom you work for. The two may be connected, but the two are never the same. You are not who you work for. Your business card tells the world who you are and explains how you can assist your new contact.

Your card should be a great representation of you. Be proud of your business card. Whether you realize it or not, you are God's gift to someone, not everyone, but someone in particular. Your financial growth and peace is associated with how well you are able to connect yourself with those who need you. A solid business card is a great way to publish yourself and make important connections.

7. Good Websites Are A Must

As a result of the social networking and the Internet explosion, everyone with a career can have a website – a virtual office. The Internet has made it incredibly easy to have a global presence, where you can connect with friends, colleagues, and customers. Everyone with a career should have an electronic home.

Having a website today is nearly comparable to having a mobile phone and an email address. As technology moves, we must move with it, in order to attract customers and stay connected to potential opportunities. Making your website attractive may require a small investment, but your website will say a lot about you and the quality of your work. Therefore, it's ok to spend a little money on marketing.

Stay ahead of the technological advancements. Society will migrate from one form of technology to another in the years to come. Anyone seeking to stay connected can quickly become obsolete by not being accessible through preferred modes of communication and information. Being too cautious or too slow to connect electronically could result in the loss of social and financial reward. Look for new ways to connect; your efforts in this area will usually pay off big dividends over time.

8. Increase You Income Goals

As your appetite grows for more career achievement, so will your financial goals. As you perfect your craft and your career, you should naturally and simultaneously position yourself for higher income. Generally, you will "not" find what you are "not" looking for. Are you pursuing higher income? You must actively search for it.

Planning your income goals is essential to actually obtaining your income goals. Further, when you've planned your financial goals, it has a way of placing everything else you do in perspective. It provides meaning and support for the decisions that you'll make in the future.

For example, if your goal is to increase your income by 20%, it may require that you obtain an advanced degree or an advanced license or certification. Let's say you're in the nursing field and you're an LPN (licensed practical nurse), a great way to achieve more income is by obtaining the RN license. Rocket science, right? You may find yourself moving from employer to employer for more income, when you actually need a higher license, a larger building, better equipment, or a marketing, or booking agent.

Changing your income preferences periodically will cause you to develop a stronger career. Don't be afraid of the challenge. Your limitations are usually superficial barriers. See yourself reaching your financial goals and it will only be a matter of time before you actually realize those financial goals.

9. Attend Professional Meetings

Examples of professional meetings would include any meeting where you may be able to make a connection or gain information which could positively impact your career. These meetings might include town hall meetings, zoning meetings, political meetings, civic organizational gatherings, chamber of commerce meetings, school board meetings, health and wellness meetings, fundraisings, symposiums or various community-related meetings.

Attending meetings of this nature ensures that you are aware of challenges and opportunities. Integrating yourself with your immediate environment will develop your professional antennae's and allow you to better serve your community.

The success of your career depends upon how well you integrate yourself with potential customers and opportunities. A visit down to your local government and the local community offices will assist you with the dates and times of some of the community meetings in your area.

10. Keep An Updated Résumé

There are several items that you should always have updated and handy. A resume, curriculum vita, cover letter, and a listing of current references are tools that you'll always need to keep updated. You want to keep these items, just as you would a fire extinguisher or a box of ban-aids. It's only a matter of time before you'll need them. Always be prepared.

Having good interviewing skills, knowledge of your personality profile, and a keen understanding of your interests will be invaluable when the time comes to sell yourself, your product or your service.

Be able to express the value of your full person and your knowledge. Ignore fictitious cultural limitations. Black is beautiful. White is lovely. Red is wonderful. Brown, yellow, blue, and all other ethnic colors are special and all created by God. Be proud of who you are and what you bring to the table.

After all, no one is any particular color anyway. I've never actually seen a white person or a red person. I learned my colors long ago, and later realized that so-called skin color is man's poor construct for establishing superficial barriers on the mind. Rise beyond cultural limitations that have nothing at all to do with your intellectual capacity to serve humanity. In the federal government of America, a middle-eastern man is considered white, while some refer to a native American man as red – the Latinos are considered brown. This all makes absolutely no sense, though many take pride in this senseless coloring system.

Irishmen were scorned in early American history. Jews were scorned in German history. Africans were scorned in international history. Native Americans experienced great challenges in the development of the U.S. Every culture shares aspects of history that are shameful and challenging to discuss at times.

But remember, if you're an expert in your field, nothing else seems to matter; all things can be overcome. Be the best!

LIFE LESSON 9
Perfect Your Personal Performance

1. Understand the Company's Vision and Mission

Every company should have a vision and mission statement. It should be the heartbeat of every company. Read the vision statement often; learn it; know it. To the extent that you can embrace the vision and mission, you will be better positioned for advancement.

Promotion is virtually impossible for those who are not somehow able to align themselves with the mission of the company. It is absolutely vital that you align your performance with the direction of the company, even if you own the company. If for some reason you are not prepared to align your life's mission with that of your company, you should quickly pursue a company, which shares your personal mission in life.

2. Write Your Own Personal Vision and Mission

It may be difficult for you to align yourself to another's vision and mission, if you are not sure about your own. Know what and who you are called to serve.

Everyone has a personal and professional charge. Know the problem that your life was created to solve. You have a major goal that you were created to reach, which will also bring you joy and fulfillment. You must package that goal in a word or a sentence.

My personal vision statement is "turning the hearts of mankind back to God, so that we can enjoy more life". Nothing seems to work well if it's being misused or operating contrary to the manufacturer's instructions. Neither will you enjoy complete fulfillment while operating outside of your Creator's intentions. Surprisingly, we're somehow able to live our entire lives completely apart from our designer's intentions.

My purpose is to help you re-connect to your Creator and Designer in such a way that your life, purpose and divine plan becomes crystal clear to you – even to the extent that it yields you success and enjoyment. My personal mission is "to train, counsel, and instruct as many as I can by speaking, writing and producing self-help resources".

You too have a vision and mission. You'll need to prepare it and write it, if you haven't already. Your vision statement should be a statement of your life's purpose. It is what you are to perpetually work to accomplish. It is the "what" of your life. It is usually too large to be accomplished in a single lifetime. More importantly, it is a general direction or trajectory in which your life should travel.

A mission statement is the daily process or functions you use to reach your vision. This statement is the "how" for reaching your life's vision. Every life has a what, a cause, a purpose. At the same time, every life needs a "how" – a specific plan of action – a plan for "how" you are to accomplish your "what" – your vision.

I have given you my vision statement, which is to help you enjoy life as you turn towards your Creator for instructions. And, my mission statement is in essence to produce oral, written, audio-visual, coaching, and consulting products and services to assist men and women in reaching their God-given potential.

Now, prepare your vision and mission statements and you will find your life's purpose begin to take shape and motion. If you want to move a step further, then establish your "why" by discovering what's most important to you in life. This list is called your core values. Show me your listing of what is most important to you and I will show you a listing of why you are uniquely called to serve your vision.

3. Journal Your Thoughts & Ideas

One of the most important secrets to success is journaling. Unlike a diary or a to-do list, a journal is a record of ideas, notions, and opportunities that you jot down in order to keep tune with your inner self. At the core of your inner being is the energy that keeps your heart beating. It is the glow in your eye. It is the part of you that is connected to the Creator – it is your spirit. That part of you is always attached to who you are and where you should be going and what you should be doing. It is your inner compass. That part of your being is also known as your conscience. It always knows the right way that you should go. That little voice inside of us speaks all the time, however, we seem to regard so little of that voice. From now on, begin to write (in that journal) what is right for you and study it from day to day. You will find yourself on the right path over time, as you choose to record your thoughts, prayers, and ideas.

4. Read Your Job Description Regularly

When working in a position, you should always strive to fulfill the purpose for which you were hired. As simple as it may sound, reading the job description on a daily to weekly basis helps provide focus. It will enable you to spend time on what's important and not waste time on things that are not important.

Find the job description to your current position. Take a highlighter and a pen and create an outline of the top 3-5 goals of your job or career. After doing so, spend 80% of your work hours doing those things only. As you do so, you will find one of two things occurring. You will either find that you have been spending time doing the wrong things, or you will find that you job has actually changed.

If your job has changed, you should discuss the changes with your leaders. Ask for a new job description or ask that your workload be adjusted to accomplish the tasks for which you were hired. Occasionally, there may be opportunities to discuss salary adjustments.

Maintaining focus is vitally important. Focus is only focus as you narrow the perspective to refine what's absolutely important. Once your scope has been focused or narrowed, then you must narrow where you spend your time. Out of the 3-5 goals, you should further focus on 1 to 2. One can excel only with focused activities. Excessive multi-tasking is not effective for anyone.

It is very difficult to maximize your performance, if you're not sure what you were hired to do. You can only be sure of what is written – the job description. Your job description is somewhat of a contract between you and your employer. Focus on fulfilling that contract. If you are able to deliver more than what is expected then once again, you will position yourself for advancement, but ensure that you've mastered what is required for evaluation.

5. Understand the Power of Teamwork

Teamwork is one of the most incredible forces known to man. From a team of horses pulling a carriage, to a team of animals pulling a sled, to a team of staff members pulling together for a project, appreciate teamwork. You'll find that it is one of the most powerful forces of any company. Unfortunately, not everyone views "team" in this way. Sometimes, it is overemphasized and other times it is terribly underemphasized.

There are many times when work should be done alone. However, don't make the mistake of becoming too independent. *Independence requires the support of many*. No one is truly independent. From the equipment one uses to the education one has amassed to the financial support it requires to pay a salary, it will always take more than one person to get a job done well. Independence is terribly overrated.

There is a measure of loss when the full weight of a team is not integrated. Let's take a restaurant for example. Imagine the restaurant's manager, who is the cook, who is also the waiter. In an effort to keep labor costs low, eventually quality and customer satisfaction will suffer from too much responsibility.

You will make more costly errors working alone than by invoking the support of a team. Notice, I did not say you will make more errors. You may, in fact, make fewer errors, but the errors you will eventually make could be the most costly and time-consuming errors. The reason is because once we get into a routine, it is difficult to see potential errors outside of your routine. It's called tunneled vision. Once you get inside the tunnel, you can't effectively see outside of that tunnel. Teamwork creates a defense both inside and outside of the tunnel.

Without teamwork, employees become stuck inside of the work tunnel with little to no help. Although employee job security appears to be stronger without teamwork, the security of the entire organization is more at risk without teamwork. Without teamwork, the organization produces employees who are overworked, frustrated and unhealthy. Teamwork, on the other hand, provides a shield against the negative effects of having certain organizational roles understaffed.

Be a voice and a champion for teamwork and your organization will produce more, earn more, and perhaps provide longer life for your company's employees.

6. Maintain Balance [Family-Health-Work]

Your health is usually sandwiched between significant responsibilities, such as family and work. It is vitally important that you learn to increase your performance with family and work by increasing emphasis upon your mental, physical and spiritual health. With emphasis on these three levels of health, you can secure and maintain your balance, as you walk the tight rope of life.

7. Follow The 8 P's of Personal & Business Development

The 8 P's of Development are in essence eight stages that any person or business must encounter in order to reach a very high level of peace and satisfaction with work and life. In the following diagram, consider the questions. Begin to systematically work your way through each question. Be mindful that it may take years to effectively answer and satisfy each question. So, be patient with yourself as you go through this developmental process.

THE 8 P'S OF
Personal & Business Development

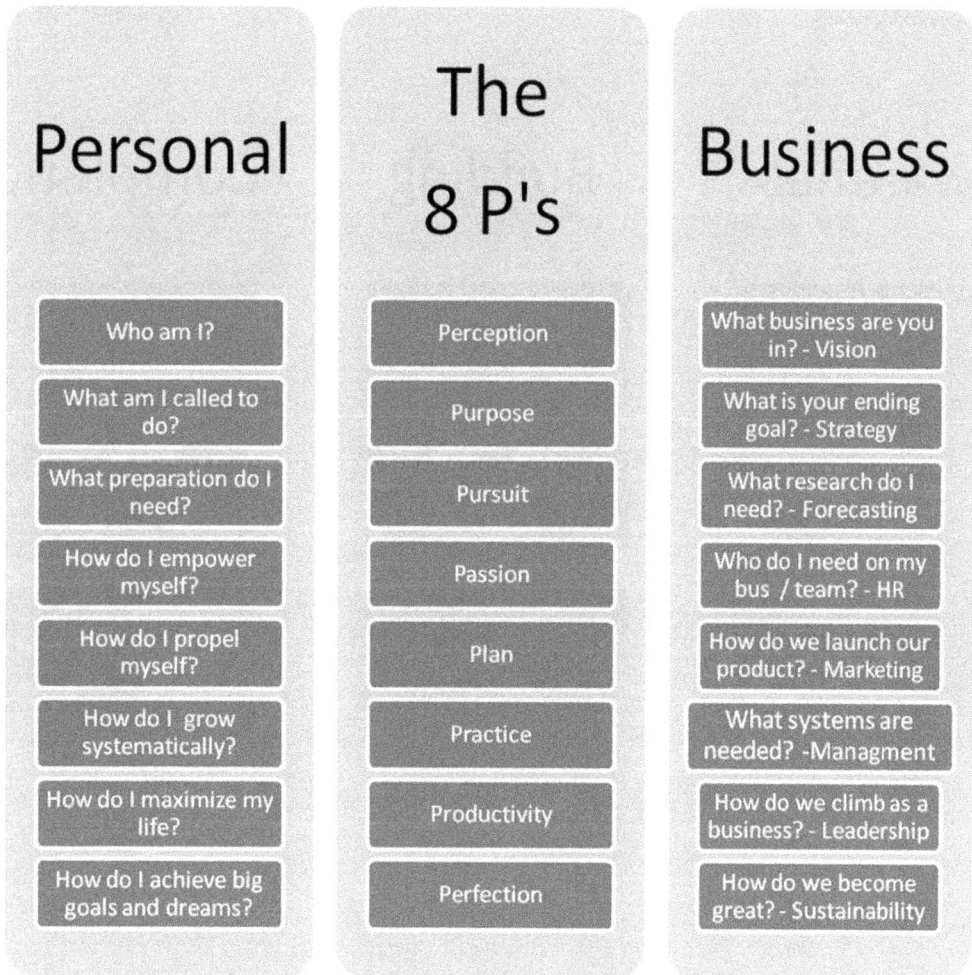

Personal	The 8 P's	Business
Who am I?	Perception	What business are you in? - Vision
What am I called to do?	Purpose	What is your ending goal? - Strategy
What preparation do I need?	Pursuit	What research do I need? - Forecasting
How do I empower myself?	Passion	Who do I need on my bus / team? - HR
How do I propel myself?	Plan	How do we launch our product? - Marketing
How do I grow systematically?	Practice	What systems are needed? -Managment
How do I maximize my life?	Productivity	How do we climb as a business? - Leadership
How do I achieve big goals and dreams?	Perfection	How do we become great? - Sustainability

It is extremely important that you challenge yourself, your business idea or existing business by thoroughly answering each question. Through this process, I strongly recommend that you hire a professional life coach to assist you.

Coaching employs an ingenious art of meticulous questioning, which allows you, the client or business owner, to come to certain conclusions that you may not otherwise be able to obtain.

In the Preface of this book, you'll find that this diagram connects with the **A,B,Cs of Dream Development**. You'll also find that the questions of the **8 P's of Personal and Business Development** are worded a bit differently than the questions of the A,B,Cs of Dream Development to provide greater perspective. **It's Time** to develop yourself, your business - your dreams. For additional support, complete the companion workbook for Lesson 9 or contact our office for personal or group coaching. Wait no longer. It's Time.

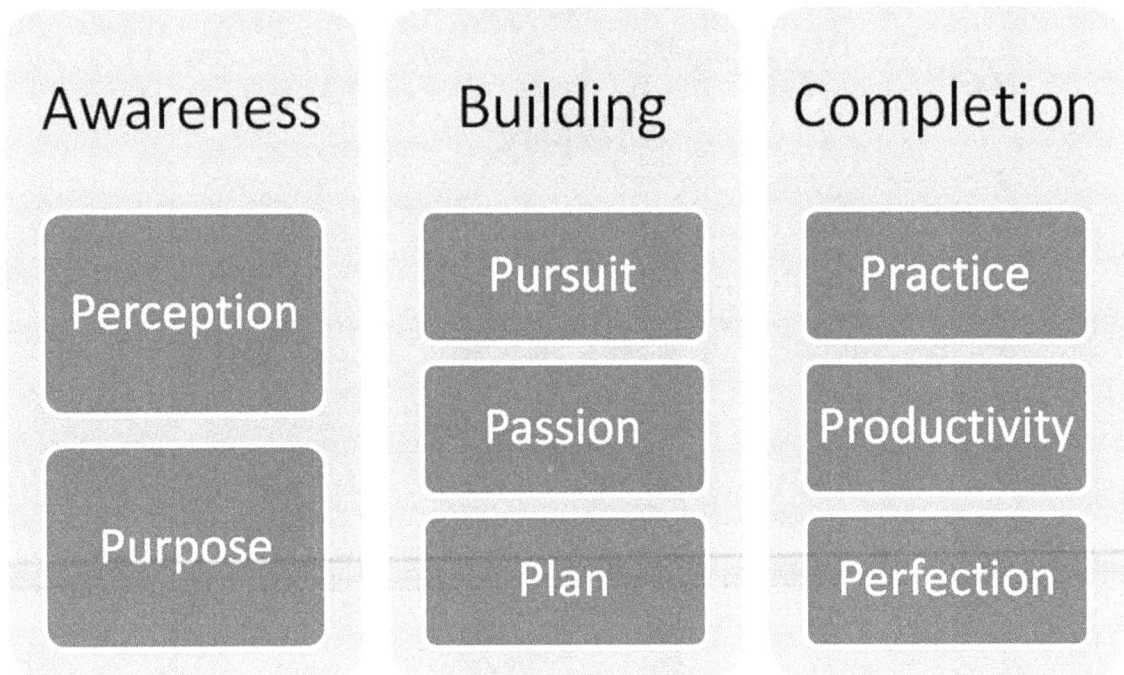

Awareness

Perception

Purpose

Building

Pursuit

Passion

Plan

Completion

Practice

Productivity

Perfection

MASTER KEY # 3
Pursue Financial Health

Social Security may not be available to Generations X, Y, or Z. As Baby Boomers begin to draw on social security benefits, allocated resources seem to simultaneously evaporate. This issue once talked about becomes a startling reality. What a wake-up call to the upcoming generations. There is only a 20-30 year span before the GenX'ers begin to retire. If social security becomes a distant reality, how will we live? How will you retire? If our health begins to fail during our 60s and 70s while the age of social security rises from 62 to 70+, are we prepared to work every day up to the age of 70? One of the federal proposals against the dwindling Social Security Retirement Fund is to not allow Americans to draw upon their social security funds, until we are closer to death - potentially eliminating the need to refund these retirement funds. We may be able to draw upon a 401k or IRA a little sooner, but will these funds be enough on which to retire? Allow me to put it this way. With the coming decades, we may see more of the elderly fall victim to sudden poverty. As inflation rises and our economy stumbles, I urge you to not place your entire lives in the hands of an uncertain governmental retirement system.

> *As inflation rises and our economy stumbles, I urge you to not place your entire life in a governmental retirement system.*

It's Time to take your finances very seriously. It has been said that most Americans are only one paycheck away from poverty. It is very important for us to get debt and spending under control, so that we can begin saving for college and preparing for later years. Speaking of college, if you are dependent upon the government to pay for your child's college with the Pell Grant, don't bank on it. The Pell Grant is too at great risk. It is absolutely vital that today's family begin increasing income, savings and investments, if you're looking for greater financial security with the coming times.

Generally speaking, Americans have very little savings, little to no investments, no financial plan for independence, and small individual retirement accounts (IRA). Many employers have sponsored retirement plans, but please be shrewd about those, as companies who go bankrupt or who have shoddy retirement plans could still render you empty handed at the end of the day. You may recall my father's story of working with a major textile company for 33 years. Between you and me, his monthly pension is much smaller than he anticipated. And, many of his coworkers lost all of their company retirement via company bankruptcy. Luckily, he got out just in time. I have four words for you. This is serious business.

The good news is this. If you are reading this book, you still have time to prepare. You can take the necessary steps to totally remove yourself and your family from future poverty. But, this simply cannot occur until you decide to begin taking responsibility for your financial health.

Anyone can develop a financial plan for wealth. It does require a fair amount of financial knowledge to prepare a solid plan. More importantly, you will need the ability and discipline to execute your plan. Start by taking a closer look at where you want to go. The following lessons are recommended to achieve financial health.

MONEY, MATTERS OF THE HEART

Money matters are heart matters.
Irresponsibility ruins lives,
Leaving young men and women in tatters.

Money matters are heart matters.
Broken dreams of children and grandchildren,
Are we the reason opportunity shatters?

Money matters are heart matters.
The next generation won't need a lecture,
They'll need your savings; healthy money ladders.

– Joe McDaniel

LIFE LESSON 10
3 Steps To Reaching Your Financial Goals

Step One

Have a family meeting. Jot down where you want to be financially in 1 year, 5 years, 10 years and 20 years. Label it, **Financial Goals & Dreams**. It doesn't need to be sophisticated; simply write out your financial goals and place them in a personal file.

Step Two

Now that you know where you want to go financially, begin building a road map. In order to do that, your second step is to determine where you are. You'll need 3 things: 1) A family budget (indicating whether you're in the red or black), 2) a statement of net worth (indicating your assets versus your liabilities), and 3) a will (indicating how you plan to allot your possessions). You will be able to find these forms in the It's Time Workbook or you may download them from my website.

    a.   **A Family Budget** will allow you to see where your money is going and allow you to determine how you'll begin growing a financial future. Please know that existing on a month-to-month basis is much different than growing your financial farm. In your budget, you'll simply take a very close look at your outgoing and incoming finances to see if you're in the red or the black. If you're in the red, you can begin charting a path for having a monthly surplus by making cuts – cut cable, refinance the home, sell the car and drive a car that's paid, reduce the cell phone package, buy groceries instead of dining out, getting a part-time job, cut your own hair, mow your own lawn, wash your own car, etc, etc – until things change.

When your budget reaches the black or, if you're already in the black, you can begin earmarking your surplus towards things that really matter. Begin by increasing your net worth, developing a college fund, investing in mutual funds, starting a small business, increasing savings, or securing other appreciating assets like gold, or rental property. Once you activate this step, you're well on your way to financial success. Regardless of how small your savings and investments are, simply get started and remain consistent, and you will begin to grow solid assets. You can arrive on the brighter side of your financial life if you make a decision to go there.

b.   **A Statement of Net Worth** is an instrument that you will need in order to determine your cash value at this moment in time. It determines whether you're worth a positive cash amount or a negative cash amount and to what degree. This instrument will allow you to examine everything you own, which can be turned into cash (assets), and everything that still needs to be paid off in full (liabilities).

In life, we have no choice but to build and develop our own financial dreams. Realize that if you fail to be proactive with your finances, dreams will naturally dismantle, as with any dollar that has no purpose. It somehow evaporates. It is important to give every dollar you earn a name and a purpose. After completing your net worth statement, go back and revisit your Financial Goals & Dreams on a monthly basis and repeat Step One on a monthly basis, until you reach your financial goals.

c.   **A Will,** though very necessary for household order, is an additional opportunity for you to get up close and personal with the value and estate that you have built for your family thus far. Rather than seeing this as an opportunity to plan final arrangements, see this more so as a chance to drastically change the legacy that you will leave for your children and your grandchildren. In fact, see this as an opportunity to project the financial impact that you want to make on your community, your church, your favorite charity, college or university. Your life is an opportunity given by God to propel the next generation a little further through the planning you are doing right now. Rather than shun this opportunity to face the sum of your life today, embrace this opportunity to advance the sum of your life. Any attorney can assist you with planning a will. But more importantly, plan a mock will for the legacy that you will leave in 30-50 + years.

d.   **Develop A Plan** – Now with a budget, financial statement, and will in place, you are prepared to make adjustments based upon that information. If there's a budget deficit or if you're in the red with your budget, then you'll simply need to make substantial cuts for the sake of your overall financial dream. If you have made cuts and there's simply not enough income, then you must plan to increase your income to the point where you have enough to begin building assets, building a legacy to pass on, and funding your future. You cannot create a plan without good data. Step Two (a,b,c) consists of the data components needed to develop your plan. In the end, there will be nothing at all complicated about your plan. The plan, simply put, is an informed direction needed to reach your goals. It's not difficult, but it requires the following step, which is the most difficult for many of us.

Step Three

Do It. Execution is one of the most important and omitted steps of any plan. If you don't actually engage these two steps none of this will work for you and you will find yourself in the same or worse positions year after year. Find a reason to Do IT. If your peace of mind does not compel you, find a reason of significance – perhaps your spouse, your children, your family, your nieces or nephews, your church, your community. There must be a reason, a why, that causes your efforts to build a financial structure worthwhile. Find your "why" and do it – make the plan. If you can only find a large enough why, your why will find the how.

There is much work ahead of you, and the more you ignore true work for your family, the more difficult it will become to reverse a negative net worth. Many Americans have negative net worth, due to high mortgage debt, second mortgages, student loans, high credit card balances, and multiple car loans. Monthly cash generating assets are certainly in the minority with American households.

An asset is something that puts money into your pocket monthly and a liability is something that takes money out of your pocket on a monthly basis. Most American families fail to realize that their prize possession, their home, is actually a liability (debt), because the mortgage actually takes money out of their pockets on a monthly basis, unless you choose to move and rent it. Most financial planners will not consider your home a true asset because few will sell their home to pay off smaller debt and your personal home does not generate cash for you on a monthly basis. Moreover, others of you may consider your employment to be an asset. But remember, an asset is only something that you can cash can cash-in, liquidate, or receive cash flow from.

In the game of financial success, it is extremely important that you learn to have more cash makers than cash takers.

While your employment can assist in purchasing assets, it is not an asset because it cannot be sold for cash. **In order to grow wealth, it is extremely important that you learn to have more cash makers than cash takers**. Anything that requires cash from your pocket every month is a cash taker. Anything that returns money to your pocket every month is a cash maker. Does money grow on trees? No. But, money does grow, if you create a little money farm using small investments for that money tree. The only way to grow money is to invest in the virtual money tree. Begin with the seed of an investment – a lawn service, yard sale, a craft or talent – it all begins with a seed of an idea. Plant more money trees in your home and never cut them down after they grow.

Further, as you grow your income begin to grow wealth by applying any surplus income on your liabilities, which would eventually eliminate debt. Once all debt has been cleared, refrain from additional debt and begin aggressively purchasing assets. Let's recap on what I've just mentioned.

 a. Balance your budget.
 b. Create Income Streams - part-time jobs, mini-businesses, garage/yard sale, creative /intellectual property, develop products and services that you can package for sell.
 c. Begin paying off debt to become debt free - start with the smallest loans first. Once each is paid off, take the extra income and pay off the next smallest loan, and so on.
 d. Once debt free, create your own bank. Develop savings and an emergency fund, college fund, new vehicle fund, and general savings for future purchases.
 e. Purchasing assets (good stock, bonds, mutual funds, CDs, business equipment, property, products to sell, or even a academic degree or certification for higher monthly income.)

The key is thinking as a producer and not a consumer. Instead of looking to buy everything, seek to sell anything – anything that holds you down or that can become an income stream. Families who build wealth have the ability to generate income and accumulate more than they spend. This is the outlook needed to revolutionize your financial life. Trust me, anyone who is financially successful, practice these simple tips.

LIFE LESSON 11
Unravel the Mystery of Investments

Play the Investment Game

There is primarily one thing to remember with any investment – Profit. As you know, gross profit is the difference between your costs (what you paid) and your selling price (your return). Among many things, there are 4 ways to achieve profits.

1. **Purchase a product (anything)** - at a very low price. Then, **sell the product** later for a higher price. From eBay, to Craig's List to flea markets to yard sales to investing in cars and houses, if you are seeking to make an investment and you have the money saved, you can make a profit and increase your household income by selling virtually anything. Normally, a little fix up or small repair is all that is required.

2. **Purchase company stock.** Stock trading is based upon the previous and timeless principle of buying low and selling high. A good stock purchase is a tiny certificate of company ownership, which increases in value as the company increases performance and becomes more profitable. The key to success in purchasing stock is knowing an industry well enough to know which companies will be in high demand in the future. From commodities such as gold, silver, corn, wheat, and oil to sector stocks such as, banking, pharmaceuticals, and technology to penny stock, which has an extremely low purchase price, there are many options for purchasing stock.

   If you choose not to sell your stock and hold it for several years later, you could be paid periodically, in the form of dividends. Dividends are in essence small appreciation checks for being part owner in the company.

   Another later purpose for purchasing stock is for trading stock for profit. For example, let's say you've purchased 1500 shares of a pharmaceutical stock for $1 per share. You've spent $1,500. After a period of time, let's say the stock rises in value to $3 per share. You then sell or trade all 1500 shares of your stock to another buyer for 3 dollars per share at a total price of $4,500. Your return or gross profit is $3,000.

   With any stock, there is also a risk of losing your money if the company performs poorly or worse goes out of business. For example, if our stock goes down in value to 50 cents per share, then our

$1,500 investment becomes $750 – half of our initial investment. You would lose money, unless you choose to hold the stock until its value returns to $1 per share. So, it pays to hire a stock expert, as you read and conduct your own research of each company's history and stock performance.

3. **Purchase mutual funds.** Mutual funds are collections of stock that are purchased and managed by a private company of stock experts. The benefit of a mutual fund is that you are able to rely upon someone else who thoroughly understands the world economics better than you. Mutual fund managers will understand which products or companies will be making the most money for you. The fund manager is an expert who makes your stock purchases and manages your stock purchases for you and thousands of others who have mutually pooled their money together so that the fund manager can invest for everyone as a single unit. You should choose a mutual fund which has a long history of returning at least 10% - 15% annual profit – or return. With a mutual fund, the risk of losing your money is significantly lower than purchasing stock directly from a company on your own because all eggs are not invested into one basket. So, if one company goes bankrupt, it negatively effects only a small percentage of the funds total investment. And, because the mutual fund is well diversified, they are generally as safe as the overall state of the economy – which is hopefully strong and growing profitably.

4. **Purchase bonds, or bank CDs.** Bonds and CDs (Certificate of Deposit) offer the least amount of risk for loss. However, the rates of return or profit are significantly lower than higher performing stocks, which can pay much higher returns. It is generally a good idea to not place all of your investment funds in one basket. In other words, use a portion of your investment pool to purchase a portion of stock, a portion of bonds, CDs and perhaps other products, such as real estate. Or, in other words, diversify your investments in all five areas mentioned in this section. Again, although the returns of these two instruments are lower than public stocks and higher than normal bank interest, the risks of loosing your money are historically lessened. The primary caveat is that if you want to withdraw your money from the instrument to use it early at some point, there is commonly a stiff monetary penalty for doing so.

5. **Purchase raw materials or assemblies.** Perhaps you are good at creating, or building, or baking, or assembling something crafty. In order to create or to assemble something wonderful and useful to others, you would need to purchase the necessary sub items, so that you can sell your finished product at a much higher price. Unlike number 1, where you've purchased a finished or turnkey product, you are manufacturing in this case. Manufacturing can be very lucrative, when the demand for what you're creating is high and your costs to produce the product are low. Fundamentally, every manufacturing business operates under the same concept – keeping supply and operational costs as low as possible, while selling their products for the highest possible price.

Small Glossary of Investment Terms

The Rule of 72 – The rule of 72 indicates how long it takes for an investment to double. For example, productive stocks may range from 5% to 18% rates of return annually. Let's say you purchase private company stock, which normally has an annual growth rate of 16%. Now, 16% is a bit higher than the stock market, but we'll use an aggressive example just to demonstrate the rule.

To compute the amount of time it will take your investment to double, you would divide 72 by the interest rate - in this case 16. After calculation, we learn that it would take 4 ½ years for your investment to double.

Let's say you have $10,000 laying around in a checking account or you sell a piece of property and acquire $10,000. Here's a quick scenario. If you placed those funds in an investment account in stocks yielding 16% annually, theoretically, you would have $20,000 at the end of 4.5 years. It would double. If you left it all in for another 4 ½ years, you would then have $40,000, so on and so on. Imagine a nine-year-old child on his way to college. At age 13, the child will have $80,000 in the college fund. At age 18, the child would have $160,000 in their college fund. All you invested was $10,000. Compound interest and a careful eye did all the work. This works the same way for a retirement account or a vacation home down the road.

How do you get the first $10,000? By setting priorities, waiting on the new car and driving the older paid off car. Payments on two new cars are easily $10,000 a year. It's a frame of mind geared toward producing a dollar instead of spending a dollar.

Here's what's even more astonishing about compound interest. Let's say you sacrifice new furniture (a bill, any bill) and a bunch of credit card purchases to allow an extra $500 per month to be added to these funds. You could add $6000 per year to the investment pot. To make a long story short, I'll do the math for you. You would have approximately $320,000 after 18 years of investing at 16% and adding only $500 per month to the pot. In essence, you will have doubled it all again from $160,000 to 320,000 by reinforcing the investment with additional monthly investments. Isn't that amazing? Even if you choose not to make a dime interest and choose a savings account instead, your own money would total $118,000. Well, that's not a bad college fund for one child. But, if you have four children like me, take the exact same amount of savings and invest it for triple your investment after 18 years. This example at 10 or 12 percent return is still very attractive.

Compound Interest In essence, compound interest is the process of continuously rolling over your interest earned to create larger and larger principal amounts. In other words, your principal investment is making interest for you; then, your new interest earned is added to the original principal investment for a new and larger principal (or compounded) to make more and more interest for you, as it all continuously rolls over, as long as you like. Traditionally, this has worked for banks and creditors to make them very wealthy. As a debtor, your debt would create more and more debt. However, as an investor, your interest profits would create more and more interest profits. Compound interest - same instrument, different side of the table.

Portfolio Your assortment of stock purchases is called a **portfolio**. The term portfolio basically refers to the collection of documents, which represent each of your current purchases.

Dow Jones – Charles Dow and Edward Jones developed an industrial average, which indicated the productivity and performance of the stock market, based on the company's performance of 30 or more top companies trading stocks. The Dow Jones is an indicator of how well the overall stock market is doing. A line graph over time or the up or down tickers for the Dow Jones is helpful in deciphering the state of the market.

S&P 500 - This is a listing of the 500 top traded U.S. based companies and their stock prices. These companies may be traded on either the NASDAQ or the New York Stock Exchange. This grouping is helpful when identifying top performers and companies with strong capital. **Capital** basically means the amount of cash and resources a company has on hand.

NYSE – New York Stock Exchange One of the two major stock trading markets in the U.S. The NYSE is located at 11 Wall Street, Manhattan, New York. At this location, you will find somewhat of a store or an auction house selling massive chunks of company stock to investors, who in turn offer the stock to you, often through mutual funds.

NASDAQ – The second of the two major trading markets in the U.S. The NASDAQ is located in Times Square, New York.

Bull Market – A bull market is somewhat of a nick-name for a period of time when stock purchasing and stock market confidence is high. An increase in the number of stock purchases or trades will be taking place during this time. Investor's are seeking to more aggressively buy stock during this period of the economy.

Bear Market – A bear market is the opposite of the bull market. I suppose it's taken from the animal that goes into long retreats or hibernation from purchasing. Investor confidence and money becomes more limited, usually due to economical trouble, political confusion, or massive industrial glitches. Stock trading overall begins to slow down in a "bear market".

Flat Market – Occasionally, you may hear this term. It means that the overall trading of stocks is consistent. You will not see a steady upward spike of growth in the bull market, nor the steady decline in trading and spending with the bear markets. There is little to no volatility.

Volatility - the level of volatility indicates the level to which a stock or market can quickly go up or down in terms of trading volume. The more volatility the market has, the more risk you have of losing money, due to instability – losses or dips in volume and stock prices.

Hedge Fund - A Hedge fund is similar to a mutual fund in that it pools the resources of many. It differs from mutual funds in that it is only open to very wealthy, skilled investors and fund managers who are experts in purchasing troubled stocks, stocks of companies with high debt and high risk, but have increased promise at the same time. In other words, hedge funds use very creative and aggressive means for making profits, regardless of the state of the economy or the state of the stock market. Hedge funds actually thrive on volatility and making extremely expensive gambles. Big risk generally means either big payoff or big loss.

Rate of Return - The rate of return (ROR) or the (ROI) return on investment is that which is returned to you above your initial investment. It would be the same as profit. The amount of return maybe identified as percentage or what may be called margin – profit margin, which is another term to describe percentages of profit.

Equity – Equity is a term primarily used in real property. It is another interesting word for profit. If you purchase a home for $50,000 and the (market) value of the home is actually $100,000, then there is $50,000 equity or profit imbedded into the home. If you decide to sell or liquidate it, you could quickly cash-out profit through selling or flipping such properties. If you have credit worthiness or enough savings to make an investment in real property, you can sometimes find these good purchases, which will yield a significant profit.

Master Key # 4
Ensure Family Wholeness

When understanding the family and learning how to develop domestic success, we must first examine the father's role in the home or the defining voice which helps shape the success of the family. In our American tradition, the bride doesn't propose to the groom, but the groom proposes to the bride. The family doesn't take on the bride's name, but the groom's name. The burden is not traditionally upon the bride to support the family, but ultimately upon the groom. The male has both the burden and the responsibility (given by God) to protect, profuse, provide, and produce for the family. Man has been given authority (by God) to help direct the family. If he's a smart man, he will learn to do this in harmony with his wife and children.

God's design for family structure began with Adam, then Eve (his bride), and then their offspring. A family, which operates outside of God's order, will see cyclical challenges. Christ, a servant and sacrifice, gave himself for the family of God, as the groom to his bride – the church. There is a correlation between Christ, the head of the church and man, the head of the family. Even in the wild of nature, you will find similar family structures of the male, the female, and the offspring, operating as a cohesive unit. In many ways, Jesus Christ is a fatherly example, as the head of his family – the church.

The role of the groom, the father and head of the family is to sacrifice himself (his time, his talent, and his treasure) for the family. Further, the role of the father is to serve the family with the highest quality of love and devotion possible. Finally, the role of the father is commissioned to save the family from any foreseeable danger, economic danger, domestic danger, or spiritual danger. To sacrifice, serve and save are the roles given to the head of the family.

When the leader is out of place, it is vitally important to fill that role with some one or some thing that will sacrifice for, serve and save the family. In some cases, the fatherly replacement for the home may be a mentor, a supporting organization, the church, or surrogate family members. Nonetheless, reestablishing the role of the father as the head of the home is vital to family wholeness. Reestablish godly leadership, spiritual nourishment and holistic perspective and the body will become much healthier, stronger, and successful, as the head of the family becomes more effective.

In this section, we will examine the roles of marriage, parenthood, positive family culture, and family order. Activating the master key of family wholeness will bring increased success to your entire household. **It's Time to put your family on track for domestic success.**

Family

When everything fails, one thing remains.
The endurance of the mountain, a force that breaks chains

When everything fails, one thing stands sure
A love that will cross violent rivers, a love indeed pure

When everything fails, one thing will never fade
An ability to bounce back, with the fortitude of which steel is made

When everything fails, depend upon one thing
The most powerful entity on earth, family, symbolized in the diamond ring

- Joe McDaniel

LIFE LESSON 12
Avoid Marital Pitfalls

Declare War For Peace

The subtitle suggests that couples should fight for peace, at all costs. It's an oxymoron, but a very important strategy to domestic sanity. Peace is a state of being, where everything is calm, intact, and yet progressive. I encourage you to evaluate your marriage to determine if things are calm, intact, and progressive. If you have peace, congratulations, I'm sure you've invested much. You must continue to protect that state of peace in your home. However, if you do not have peace, declare war for peace.

To declare war for peace, you must oppose and remove anything that could attack your state of order, serenity, togetherness, and progression. As in a state of war, we must constantly be on the lookout for intruders. Intruders may be the purchase of a new toy, which will take time, attention, and money from the household budget. An intruder may be a new friend or family member requiring too much time and attention. An intruder may be too much television or too many hours at work. Guard the peace, by quickly attacking anything intruding on domestic wellness.

> *To declare war on peace, you must oppose and remove anything that could attack your state of order, serenity, togetherness and progression.*

Those who allow their peace to be trivial will slip into enemy territory and find themselves in a pitfall – a deep place of despair and disappointment. If you've found yourself in this pitfall, you will need the aid of each other and potentially a pastor, a coach or marital counselor to assist you in climbing out to a place more comfortable.

The Pit of Unforgiveness

This topic is probably one of the most painful topics to discuss because the nature of forgiving indicates emotional damage. Emotional wounds heal very slowly. And, the healing process will never begin if the wounds are concealed.

Wounds need to be exposed in order to heal. Physical wounds need air, oxygen, and the aid of a disinfectant in many cases. Emotional wounds also need to be aired, cleansed with forgiveness and released in order for healing to take place. For whatever reason, exposing an emotional wound is the most challenging. But, please understand, there is no other way for healing to occur. You must tell a healing specialist about the pain and hurt before they can assist you with the healing found in forgiveness.

Living in a state of un-forgiveness is an emotional pitfall that can rob you of the best years of your life. Consider the following steps to emotional healing.

1.   Agree with yourself to begin the healing process.
2.   Prepare to reveal the wound. Set a date, a location, and a support person whom you can confide in.
3.   Reveal the wound to yourself first. Confess your hurt out loud, then to a friend or spouse.
4.   Once the emotional wound is exposed, you must undergo a painful purging process. Allow whatever feelings of release to take its course. You may become very verbal, you may cry, you may become angry or have outbursts. But, you must get it all out.
5.   Let it go – Forgive – Release It. Don't allow that hurt to take residence in you any longer. It is a disease that will always entrap you. You are too valuable and too precious to be held captive by someone's hurt. Cancel their debt for your sake and in return repurchase your life.

> *Emotional wounds heal very slowly. And, the process of healing will never begin if the wounds are concealed.*

The following is a suggested confession: State it out loud.

"You hurt me, but I forgive you because God made me a wonderful person who has the power to forgive. I cannot afford to sell my peace in life to this pain forever. Therefore, I am releasing myself from this hurt and from this anger and walking away from it into all the peace and happiness that is waiting me. I forgive you. And, I release myself from harboring this pain inside of me. I free you and I free myself to move on in life towards happier places. I am free. I release you and drop all charges and pray that all is well with your life from this day forward. I forgive you and I forgive myself.

LIFE LESSON 13
Set Family Ground Rules

In baseball, the term "ground rules" are used to differentiate the unique rules specific to each ballpark. Baseball parks are designed uniquely from other parks, though they may appear to be the same. As a result, there are rules, which govern the game on that specific park. In the game of marriage, every marriage is different. Because every marriage is different, different rules may apply to each marriage. For example, in one marriage, the husband may pay the bills. In other marriages, the wife may pay the bills. There may be separate bank accounts between the two, and so on. These differences in marital operations are "preferences". In marriage, ground rules differ from preferences, in that they are huge anchors that keep the marriage stable.

To explain this further, I will list some of the ground rules that have aided Tish and me in successfully maintaining our short 20 year tenure in marriage.

The McDaniel Ground Rules

1. To keep our home a Christian home – no exceptions
2. To stay in love – by practicing love-like behavior – being affectionate, complimenting, improving each other, and by doing everything together. We will create an environment for love. We share plates together; we attend school together; we will do everything together.
3. To play on each other's strengths instead of fighting over our weaknesses.
4. To refrain from using the term "divorce". It is off limits – never to be used as it relates to us.
5. To refer to each other by their name only. The words "stupid" or "dumb" or "fool" or "crazy" are absolutely off limits. These are terms that we have NEVER used toward each other. For the sake of the truth, there may have been a silent slip in 20 years, but we honestly make a strong effort to not make such a terrible slip. Downgrading talk or gestures are not to be used in describing or communicating with each other.
6. To never embarrass each other - in private or public.
7. To refrain from discussing our marital concerns with friends or family – only to each other - only.
8. To never establish inappropriate extra-marital relationships. This includes friendships or best-friendships that conflict with the marriage. At this time, we only have distant friends – those we talk with once or twice a month, at the absolute most.

9. To apologize when necessary. If an apology is necessary to resolve a dispute, we always apologize at the appropriate time. Then, discuss how we might avoid future hurdles of the same nature.
10. To pray. When everything else fails, we "literally" pray, pray, pray. Generally, prayer has been our saving grace during our most challenging times in marriage. Prayer places us in a state of humility and allows us to see ourselves and the error of our ways.

These items are not minor preferences; they are solid ground rules that we've set in place to guarantee our marital success. We set them in place over two decades ago, well before we were married. Carefully review our ground rules. I think you would agree that if we held to these ground rules (and we will), we should have a successful marriage to the very end. By establishing this mutual order of respect, we are able to enforce our agreement. These rules are not extraordinarily sophisticated, but the power of agreement is most important.

LIFE LESSON 14
Decide to Agree

The best time to come in agreement is during times of garrison, or in other words, during times when you're not battling serious issues and problems. Always determine what your strategy will be before conflicts arise. A conflict strategy is a very valuable tool, but only has value during times of conflict. Therefore, when conflict occurs, you'll be extremely grateful for your conflict resolution plan.

I once heard the quote, "the best form of preparation is anticipation". Realize that if your challenge has not yet surfaced, it will surface soon. An approaching challenge in your marriage is certainly down the road, perhaps a challenge you've never before faced. If you fail to prepare for this upcoming challenge, crisis, or emergency, you will pay a dear price for being unprepared.

> *"The best form of preparation is anticipation"*
> *-source unknown*

Prepare now. Talk about a conflict resolution plan now. Plan the budget. Plan the romantic date. Plan the much-needed get away. **It's Time!** Do something now. Plan to secure additional household income for an emergency fund now. You might agree beforehand to stop spending and begin putting savings in place now. Anticipate weak links in your marriage and plan to resolve them now, while you're in garrison.

I'll briefly bear my soul for the sake of full disclosure. I once developed very serious feelings for a young lady at work. My wife was not aware of these feelings. After this problem grew to become more difficult than I could contain, I arranged a meeting and sat down with both the young lady and my wife. I had lunch with both of them together – simply to put a lid on the challenges I was facing before things got out of hand with me. They both knew the reason for the meeting and respected each other enough to grin and bear it. I anticipated a major problem in my marriage and as difficult as it was for me, I sought to clear the air by repositioning this awkward relationship. That was my crisis management plan, though I had no contingency plan before the incident. By the help of God, I proved to my wife that I was serious about my marriage. Something had to be done immediately before a "real" intimate crisis occurred.

In all honesty, had I a plan to maintain work-life balance well before the crisis, this situation would not have occurred. I never ever anticipated gaining feelings for another woman because my wife was my first girlfriend, even my very first love ever. I honestly failed to anticipate a future challenge in that area. You must anticipate possible problem areas (as bizarre as they may appear) and challenge them with a plan before they become problems. Do not wait until things occur and slip out of control. In many cases, it will be far too late to recover from a major marital attack. So be proactive.

What The Spouse May Never Tell

A spouse may never tell when she's feeling insecure.
A spouse may never tell when his heart is impure.

There are skeletons and secrets that you may never know.
A spouse may never tell every direction you must go.

Directions of the heart will seek resolve and inner peace.
In the process, inner thoughts may not be released.

There is much to wonder about the silent mind?
And, what the spouse may never tell is revealed in time.

There is one secret to knowing, for those of you who are wise,
What the spouse may never tell will be told for a special prize.

– Joe McDaniel

LIFE LESSON 15
Understand the Role of Fatherhood

Fatherhood is one of the most complicated but rudimentary relationships known to humanity. Why would I consider fatherhood complicated? The less we know about a subject the more complex it appears to be. Single-parent households led by fathers are far less common than those led by mothers. And, if there's a father in the home, the fatherly role may still seem a bit mysterious at times - unlike the common and well-known comfort of the mother's role.

In any event, to understand fatherhood, we should carefully review the origins and original intent of the Heavenly Father – our Creator, which unlocks many questions of fatherhood. I encourage you to study this topic.

Everyone has a father, right? Even with artificial insemination, there is always a father, whether known or unknown. I rarely hear the question: where are the mothers? On the other hand, I always hear the question: where are the fathers? It is incredible, how many children have never met their fathers, or have never seen their fathers. My maternal grandfather, bless his soul, walked off from the home and left his two daughters when they were one and three years of age, only to return into their lives 30 years later. It went something like this as grandma spoke to my mother: "Baby, your daddy is downtown at the bus station needing you to pick him up." My mother replied, "my daddy?", as if to say "who and what is that?" I remember, she was approximately 33 years of age and had little to no personal concept of what a daddy was. In fact, no one knew if he was alive during those 30 years or not.

This story is just a variation of countless stories from sons and daughters, many of whom have no idea of what it means to have a father in their lives. It is very sad that there is often no one at home to call dad. How has this affected our society? Incredibly, statistics has shown a tight correlation between crime, illiteracy, and poverty with the fatherless child. Though not in every case, this is all very sad, very obvious, and not the true point that I'm attempting to make.

Here's the real point that I'm attempting to make. There is another surprising phenomenon taking place in the American home today. It is the absent father who happens to live inside the home. He's there, but not there – out of touch – not relevant – applicable to certain things in the home, but not those things that concern his children and the family the most.

There is virtually no difference between this father, who is present and the father who is absent. A father who has little

> *A father who has little to no value in the home is, for all intents and purposes, an absent dad.*

to no value in the home is, for all intents and purposes, the absent dad. In other words, fathers were intended to play a role in the home. But, if the fathers, who are present in the home, do not play the proper roles, then I regret to ask, what value do they really have? How are they different from the physically absent dad?

Allow me to provide a clearer picture of the absentee dad. "I pay the bills; I come home every night, and I take out the trash - sometimes! What more can I do; what else do you want from me?" Well, I'm glad you asked. Being an absentee dad for a significant period of time myself, I am well qualified to assist.

The analytical minds of some may benefit from a detailed list of exactly what more fathers can do. Therefore, I created the following checklist needed for one to be released from the absentee dad list. Fathers, please commit to the following 12 items. I want to encourage you. You can be the father that God created you to be. And, while you come home everyday, families need more. It's Time.

12 Keys To Becoming A Better Father

1. Read & Study With Your Children

Studies show a dramatic increase in vocabulary and academic performance when reading is demonstrated and practiced along with parents versus teachers only. The responsibility of education is not the sole responsibility of the teacher, nor the government, but the parents. Fathers in particular must champion education in the home.

2. Participate In Sports & Activities

The fact that athletics and regular activities prevent childhood obesity and promote wellness is well worth our efforts in this area. Moreover, let's not forget that organized sports at early ages play an important role in childhood discipline and value setting. Sports have a unique way of developing positive values in children. Further, creating a coaching type relationship with your child creates an interesting relationship of empowerment, in terms of getting them to perform other tasks and chores. I have coached many of my four son's teams.

3. Show Affection

Showing affection is often difficult for fathers, simply because it is not accepted in the macho culture. In other words, "we don't want to make our boys soft", we say. What I have found is that boys will often mimic the dominant role in their home. If we are diligent to help them with role identification, then we would not have to worry about our boys becoming soft. Things like getting dirty, mowing the lawn, wrestling, or playing sports may help give them a balance view of humanity. A father who will not embrace his son or daughter could inadvertently force them to seek affection abnormally and elsewhere. It is critical that we teach our children the proper and healthy way to love rather than allow them to learn about love in error.

4. Teach Values and Morals

If values and morals are not taught first in the home, then children somehow feel that there are multiple standards. Ethical standards should be reinforced at home first, otherwise, standards from school, television, friends are competing. Fathers must sort out any inconsistencies. There should only be one standard of morals and values – those you live and teach by personal example.

5. Get Involved in Your Children's Ambitions

It has been said that children will discover their God-given passion in life at early ages. But, here's what's sad about that. If we as fathers have not spoken to our children enough to hear them, they cannot get the additional support and encouragement to continue sorting out their ambitions. The sorting out is what they need. Your life experiences coupled with their ambition, could possibly spark a fire in them that cannot be quenched.

6. Teach Your Sons to be Husbands

There are only a few places where a young man can learn to be a husband. He can learn from your home, his friend's home, from the television, or from on-the-job training in his own home. In looking at the four options, the first option (from your home) clearly stands out as the favorite. You may be saying, "Well, I'm not a very good example of a husband. Perhaps my son should learn from someone else." If this is your response, then you've actually supported the point that I'm about to make. Because you don't truly know everyone else, your example is just as good as anyone else's example.

No one goes into marriage with expert status as a husband. However, if you are open and transparent, a son could healthily learn from both your successes and failures. Begin investing in your son's future home now by being transparent and by taking the initiative to serve him.

7. Teach Your Daughters to be Wives

By the same token, we should also begin to explain from a husband's point of view what makes a good wife. To genuinely show them the pointers and pitfalls before they become married, even while they're young is invaluable. Fathers, you have the unique position and advantage of grooming your daughters early.

8. Talk To Them…… REALLY Talk to Them

You know, none of the aforementioned items are possible if you've not established a healthy open line of communication with your young child, teenager, or adult. I think we would be astonished to know how many fathers will not hold a 10-minute conversation with their child. This is unacceptable. Your children want to hear you affirm them, encourage them. They want us to tell them stories about our parents and grandparents. They want to hear how we handle similar challenges that they are going through. No matter the age of your child, share your life, your experiences, and your heart.

Our heavenly Father (our model of a father) says that we should talk to him without ceasing. Here it is in a nutshell. It is impossible to have any meaningful relationship with your daughter or son, if you cannot hold a conversation with them. So, let the talking begin. Go for ice cream, go for a ride – alone – and simply talk to them about whatever they want to talk about. And, if they don't want to talk, it's because you've not established and encouraged an open line of communication with them. It's Time.

9. Insist on their Absolute Best in School

In the 21st century, excellence in academics is a must for survival. Learning is a culture that you endorse or fail to endorse in your home. In other words, children have inner radars, which lets them know if you care about academics or not. If you rarely mention school, homework, or reading to them, they automatically assume that you don't care a great deal about it – even though you may occasionally inquire. Fathers, we must take an active role in placing value on education. Fathers carry a great deal of weight in the home. Let's use it for the right thing. Insist on becoming an academic partner with your child and their schools.

10. Encourage Them

There is no other encouragement in the world like a father's encouragement. Don't underestimate the value of your words, as a father. You may not get very much of a response from your children, but I can promise you that when you encourage your child, you empower them to continue to do well more than you know and more than they will tell you. My father encouraged me very little, but when he encouraged me, I knew that he meant it. It would always empower me to continue on. In fact, I'm still surprised at the feeling that comes over me when my dad tells me he's proud of me, even today. Go on; give it to them unconditionally, as only a father can. It's Time

11. Pray Over Them

Prayer teaches children many things such as humility, obedience, discipline, providence, respect, honor, love, servant hood, charity, faith, courage and the list goes on and on and on. There are dozens of attributes that we subtly teach our children when we demonstrate the ability to pray before them. If there's only one of the 12 pointers that you choose to practice, this one is absolutely the most powerful and important. Through prayer, our shortcomings are dismissed. Through prayer, our children become what they are destined to be. Speak the heavenly Father's words over your children. Words become reality. The more you speak the heavenly Father's words over them regarding their behavior, their career, and lives, the more those words would develop in them.

12. Learn from Better Fathers

Fathers, please don't get stuck in pride by assuming that you cannot learn from a real veteran. As the saying goes, the proof is in their pudding. Look for children who have excelled or who have done exceedingly well. When you find them, talk to the parents to learn a few techniques that may help you. You will do your child a great service by picking up best practices rather than carrying on poor practices.

I am convinced that if fathers took on greater responsibility in the homes, many of children's problems would be solved.

I am convinced that if fathers took on greater responsibility, such as the items listed above, many of our children's problems would be resolved. In doing so, we could change a generation through our initiative. Implementing the aforementioned items will require effort on your part, but you can do it if you try. It is not easy to change your behavior. It is not easy to correct your habits. It is not an easy thing to put away the mancho disposition to start doing what many of us may consider to be female-like chores. Remember, it is not what we're doing right that causes us to lose victories; it is what we fail to do. Can I be very honest and candid ? … Thanks

---

The reason we are the way we are is probably because we learned it from someone else, perhaps our own fathers.

- The reason I purposely hug and kiss my boys is because I never remember being hugged and kissed by my father as a child.
- The reason I work on my boys' grammar, homework, and educational interests is because I never remember my father doing any of those things with me as a child.
- On the other hand, the reason that I'm a very spiritual person is because both my father and grandfather are extremely spiritual men. I'll give my dad and granddad a check in that area. ☑

In other words, people innately become that which is modeled before them, but they later discover what was not modeled. In order for us (fathers) to change what the next generation becomes, we must model what we expect from them. We need to model the extra-mile behavior instead of inappropriate behavior, which is often what our children see. The extra-mile behavior is to care about education, even when you don't feel comfortable or adequate about education.

The extra-mile behavior is to care about education, even when you don't feel comfortable or adequate about education.

The extra-mile behavior is to do dishes, even when you feel that dishes are not your major role. If sons see fathers doing dishes, laundry, homework, and prayer in the home, they'll no longer think it's something that only wives should do.

Whatever you want your children to do as adults, model that behavior and it will likely re-appear in their adult lives.

Ever see a father sitting at a table writing out a budget? Ever see a father taking their children aside and explaining the banking statements or the investment statements of their children's educational funds? Similar observations are consistent for mothers also. Ever see a mother placing vitamins beside the father's plate or the children's plate? Ever see a mother take her children out for a walk around the track? We may not see these things very often because they were likely not modeled by our parent' parents.

Whatever you want your children to do as adults, model that behavior and it will likely re-appear in their adult lives. You cannot hope and wish that they become something that you have not modeled. You must be a good example and place them very close to good examples.

My paternal grandfather has been a deacon in church for literally 50+ years. During this period, he fathered 7 sons and 3 daughters. Out of 7 sons, 3 of them are also deacons in church, and 2 others consistently hold official positions. Out of 10 children, 9 of them devoutly participate in church on a weekly basis.

Here's another example. My great aunt-in-law retired as a registered nurse. She had 3 daughters, 2 of which are also registered nurses, while the 3rd daughter is a medical administrator. Her son is today a police officer, having followed in the footsteps of guess who, his father.

Here's one last example of the effects of modeling. My maternal grandmother lived an unmarried life after only 3 years of marriage. From the unsuccessful union of my grandfather, she had two children - two daughters - who both had one daughter each. In other words, grandmother had two daughters and two granddaughters. Today, all four are divorced and all four unmarried. In fact, out of all 5 maternal grandchildren (2 girls and 3 boys), I am the only grandchild married today.

Why? A father walked off, not to be found again for 30 years later. Think about this? What sort of value and trust did this model place on the worth of a husband and father? What became the norm, as a result of this father? In my maternal family, living unmarried unfortunately became the norm for 6 out of 7 households.

My paternal grandfather – the 87 year old deacon – has never been divorced, but married thrice due to preceding deaths. Gramp, affectionately called, loves marriage. Out of 10 of his children, 8 of them had successful marriages. My mother and father are the result of one of those broken marriages out of the 10. I spent a fair amount of time in my grandfather's home as a child, unlike my sister and cousins who may not have drawn as much from my paternal grandparent's relationship. It was always my joy to see my grandparents interact. Honestly, I think I may have modeled my paternal grandfather's marital behavior, while later avoiding the duplication of my own parent's troubled marital behavior. Two grandfather's – two totally different results.

In addition, my wife's parents celebrated their 40th anniversary a few years back. The success of my marriage is really not magic or coincidence. It's been 20 years for Tish and me now. And, we have no intentions of drastically changing things. I am truly a fan of modeling good examples.

We have all witnessed similar stories of children sharing parental successes and failures. From household cleaning patterns to professions, children are naturally inclined to follow that which has been modeled before them. Parents, who participate in crime and drugs, will inadvertently lead their children to a lifestyle of crime and drugs.

Who you are and what you do will play a role in the psychological development of others. As a father, your image will also play a major role in who your daughter chooses to marry. It will play a role in the type of husband your son will become, or, if he becomes a husband at all.

In conclusion, when you, the father, begin to lead the charge on many of the issues that count in the family, things will simply fall into place throughout your lineage.

LIFE LESSON 16
Administer Positive Discipline

Being older parents of very young children, I must say that I have much to learn about the subject of child-rearing. However, I quickly learned that if I didn't get a plan for them, they would create a plan for me. It wasn't long before the subject of discipline arose in my household. "How are we going to do this", we asked each other. Through trial and error, Tish and I developed processes. And, to my surprise, I am often told how respectful and well behaved our children are. And, while those compliments seemed like well-meaning jokes, I later realized that the comments were very sincere. I realized that others saw my children's behavior a little differently than I. In light of our small success in this area, I will mention a few of the techniques that we have implemented.

1. We never discuss any disagreements on the subject of discipline in front of the children. In fact, if we strongly disagree, we work diligently to shield the children from any contentious behavior. Do the kids need to see our disagreement? Are we being phony if we shield them? Absolutely not. There are many things that children must confront in life. But, to allow the children to see a full display of disagreement, before they have the understanding to process sharp contention can be counterproductive to their personal development, I believe.

2. Physical fighting is absolutely forbidden in our home, by anyone. Surprisingly, this must be stated in America. Domestic violence is unfortunately alive and well. Under no circumstances should any human being be subjected to physical or emotional abuse, even during discipline. If physical and emotional abuse is occurring among children or adults, it is time to find a new home with new methods for handling family affairs civilly. I have seen the affects of this firsthand, and it can ruin an emotional life. For this reason, children should be safeguarded from all abuse at all costs. Corporal punishment administered wisely and carefully is very different from abuse and can be very effective.

3. We make a point to address certain things about our disciplinary styles or the children's behavior on a regular basis. Some things cannot be avoided. Parents must talk and agree civilly about disciplinary techniques. Through conversation and prayer, we reach agreement.

4. Listen to what children are saying and what they're not saying. Regardless of age, children and youth become very reluctant to articulate strange feelings, unchartered emotions, and uncertainties about what they're facing. Occasionally, you may notice unruly behavior stemming

from hidden and very uncomfortable situations that are difficult for children to discuss. Learn to listen carefully and explore privately.

5. Build a relationship based upon love and not fear. To be loved or feared is still a current philosophical debate. Children will obviously development much better with more love than fear. They have many fears already. Fear of the parents should not be another concern of the child, but rather fear of disappointing parents, stemming from love. Effective discipline should be a product of love and care rather than fear and anger.

LIFE LESSON 17
Pursue Good Family Entertainment

There are certain forms of entertainment that are not good and there are certain forms that are very good. Movies, for example, can expose the family to intense, violent, and strong emotions that can be harmful. Some things are just not good for the soul, especially the souls of young people still in development. Many of the nightmares that children experience are from frightening movies and incredible violence. Studies have shown that anxiety disorders, fear, and phobias are the result of exposure to violent gun-filled movies and television programs with strong emotional content. Doctors have even said that many of the high impact movies playing today can affect the proper digestion of food. Who would think that intense movies could affect how the body draws nutrition. Beware of harmful movies, and have the courage to say, "this is inappropriate".

Families often view personal involvement in sports as entertainment. However, be careful with certain sports such as rugby, hockey, skiing, boxing, football, bungee jumping, and sky-diving, due the danger of getting hurt. Please be safe with dangerous recreational activities and avoid them if possible.

Research has identified brain complications from athletes having undetected concussions from as far back as 30 to 40 years. Young athletes can unknowingly obtain small concussions throughout their athletic careers. An improper fall or seemingly small accident could possibly become life threatening later on.

Entertainment from sports can be great, but physical injuries, broken bones, concussions and even arthritis can have permanent affects upon life. My caution is that you be wise with high-contact sports as entertainment and recreation. Take every precaution necessary. Encourage your athletes to stretch, train, and always wear necessary protection.

Sometimes, our athletes become entertainment for the entire family, while becoming disappointed when athletic dreams and physical injury become reality. Safeguard your children against the affects of becoming entertainers at the expense of their health and safety.

Another very popular and highly debated form of entertainment is video games – Play Station, X-Box, Wii, and other simiar gaming products. These highly stimulating forms of family entertainment can be extremely addictive and even harmful to the eyes, ears and learning patterns of children when prolonged and not monitored properly. Further, the content of such games have come under great scrutiny, as it relates to morality.

With regard to violence, the repeated firing of weapons, and the gross insensitivity and disregard for life are potentially altering the emotional compass of our consciousness. In fact, there are studies attempting to link school violence with the violence that has become common in many homes everyday, via video games. It is important to remember that some of these questionable games are not intended to be used as babysitters, but entertainment used under supervision and appropriate consumption.

Good family entertainment might include activities that you are not accustomed to. Visiting state zoos and aquariums are great entertainment. Amusement parks are excellent, but sometimes we forget about these other forms of recreation. There are many national and state parks filled with nature, historical, and educational value. Museums and educational exhibits stimulate incredible interest in the minds of the entire family. This is all good entertainment.

Any form of educational exposure can be great entertainment. For example, visiting a local airport, a local farm, or a local university can be great forms of family entertainment, which will positively connect the family to the world in which we live. Retired war ships, war airplanes, and historical military bases provide very relevant and thought-provoking entertainment. Dreams are stimulated and developed as we view history.

One of the ways that our family maintains strong bonds is by engaging in family adventures of golfing, fishing, and trail walking. If your family watches lots of television begin transitioning to the history channel, the nature channels, public and university sponsored television. These channels are much more wholesome for family development. Remember, it's never too late to begin walking in a better direction.

LIFE LESSON 18
Develop Good Family Health

Your life depends upon your health. Likewise, your family's lives depend upon the level of importance you place upon health, wellness and physical safety. If you read no other part of this section, please realize that this statement applies to 90% of the readers. Family health affects performance at work, school, and home. Family health affects your budget, your savings, and your peace of mind. Health issues can be expensive even life threatening. Your family's health is one of the most important discussions that you can have.

Healthy Eating

> *Not only do we eat the wrong things, but we eat the wrong way.*

One of the biggest culprits to poor health is poor eating. Not only do we eat the wrong things, but we often eat the wrong way. For example, the amount of time that we chew our food is often too brief for proper digestion. Proper eating isn't as simple as putting food in our mouths? Unless we know when and what to eat, we could unknowingly abuse our bodies. Allow me to address eating in two topics – when to eat and secondly, what to eat.

When to eat is a debated topic among health professionals. Traditional meal times cause a bit of confusion on the subject of when to eat. Why? Somewhere, down in history, we've developed the three-meal a day concept - morning, noon, and evening – breakfast, lunch and dinner. Or if you're in the south, it's breakfast, dinner, and supper.

Many health professionals will tell you that fasting several hours between meals is actually counterproductive to weight control and good health. As you're going throughout the day, not only do your organs require a steady stream of nutrition to function properly, but so does healthy metabolism.

We condition ourselves to wait until the next meal to eat partly for two reasons. Number one, we eat too much whenever we do eat, so we need to allow several hours for digestion. Secondly, we may feel that we're eating too often if we eat between traditional meal times.

My recommendation is to erase the concept of the traditional meal times and eat very small portions consistently throughout the day. I realize that this concept goes against everything that you were taught.

What we're battling here is culture and tradition. However, this concept is not strange at all to your bodies. Let's face it. It's our eating culture and family eating traditions that has our health in trouble.

Here's what I further recommend: Begin thinking about eating outside of normal meal times, but also rethink meal appearances. When we think about a meal, we often think about meat, bread, sides and a drink. Or, we think, one meat, two vegetables, and a dessert. The meat is likely fried or chemically processed, salty, and far too large for healthy digestion. The vegetables are likely canned, over cooked or over processed, with too little to no nutritional value. The bread is usually very tasty causing us to eat more slices, rolls, or biscuits than we should, resulting in high fat and high sugar consumption. And, if there's a salad to add the color green or to make us feel a little better, let's be honest and admit that a bowl of Iceberg lettuce adds no nutritional value to our meals.

We've adopted poor eating habits. One way to know that you've eaten poorly is if you've become sleepy shortly after the meal. There are two reasons for this sleepy feeling after eating. One, the meal might have been too large, causing your body to summons all of your energy for digestion, which zaps your brain and muscles of the energy needed to remain awake and alert. The second reason is that the starch or sugar content was so high that it sent your body into a sugar frenzy, then later balanced the upward burst of sugar with the downward plummet in energy, creating the drowsy and sleepy feeling.

Erase the meal model and adopt the healthy snack model.

It's called the "sugar drop". You may have noticed this drop after eating something very sweet. You will have a sudden burst of energy, a burst of laughter or excitement, and then a really drowsy period. This is more evident with children and lots of candy.

Back on subject, you should eat regularly and consistently throughout the day. Erase the meal system and adopt the healthy snack system. Now, I know what you're thinking. When we think of snacks, we usually think candy, potato chips, or junk food. This is absolutely not what I'm suggesting.

A healthy snack could be any of the following: a piece of fruit, an apple, grapes, a banana, fresh strawberries, plums, or a peach – whichever you like. Other snacks might include unsalted nuts, whole grains, a bottle of clean water or juice, a vegetable, slices of tomato, a few pieces of stemmed or raw broccoli (raw is always better), a few slices of cucumber, a granola bar, or fiber bar, baby carrots or steamed carrots, or a box of raisins. Get the picture. This is the food that God himself made to assist us with enjoying a full life with stabilized energy.

None of these items should drop you or hinder productivity. On the contrary, these items should give you consistent energy, so long as they're eaten in moderation. Snack a little between meetings, between classes, during breaks, and continue with your daily affairs. You should never become hungry; you should actually loose weight by increasing your metabolism; and, you should always be energetic and alert.

.....some learning challenges in children result from not only lack of education support, and poor study habits, but poor nutrition.

Allow me to take another sidebar here: Often, when children are having difficulty focusing on their studies, it is because they have eaten a poor meal. Poor meals prohibit focus and mental alertness. Do your children a big favor and ensure that they have proper eating habits, which promote learning and clear thinking.

Foods high in cheese, grease, salt, starches, and sugar can hinder learning. It terribly affects attention spans, creative thought and interferes with rigorous brain activity. I submit that learning problems in children can sometimes result from not only lack of educational support, and poor study habits, but poor nutrition.

> *Never enjoy yourself at the expense of your own health.*

Now, back to my subject – This notion of requiring a full four-course meal is cultural. The notion of wanting to be completely full after a meal is cultural and personal. As a result of culture, emotions, and recreation, we overeat. These items are the bad motives for eating.

Do not eat to get full. Do not eat for recreation or as a pastime. Eat to be energized. As a rule of thumb, food portions the size of your palm should be adequate enough to provide sufficient energy. We should strive to feel light and energetic after eating, and not heavily weighed down and tired. "I want my money's worth", is a statement you might hear at a restaurant. However, eating our money's worth will get us a lot more than we've bargained for. It will get us a doctor's visit and a pharmaceutical bill, if we're not more careful.

Never enjoy yourself at the expense of your own health. Choose other ways to enjoy yourself. Let other means of enjoyment be your hobby. Let a day out with friends, or a short trip to your favorite destination be your recreation. As you know, a good book can be very uplifting. We take far too much pleasure in eating large and unhealthy meals.

Do not make eating a main event or the highlight of the day. Make your life and the beauty of it the main event of the day, or some accomplishment the event of the day.

Consider the fueling station for a moment. Is getting fuel the best part of the trip? Getting fuel is a means to a more important end, right. Imagine for a moment, if we were cars. Would we have parties at the fuel station? Would we have ceremonies at the fueling station? Would we get so excited emotionally overwhelmed about getting more fuel, that we overfill our cars? Consider the analogy. If it were possible, I think many of us would live at the fueling station. But, think about it. How much fuel can one person hold, really? We've placed the wrong type of emphasis on the fuel needed for our bodies. It's become a cultural phenomenon.

Now, imagine a racecar, which also uses fuel, of course. For the sake of time, a racecar never makes an event at a fuel stop or pit stop. In fact, its objective is to spend as little time as possible getting fuel. Sometimes, the racecar is so in a hurry to get back into the race that it drives off without fully refueling. Allow the eating experience to be as brief as possible, so that you can get back into the race of enjoying more life.

Consider this also: The racecar has a relatively small tank, unlike humans. The racecar adopts a small tank for light, but more frequent refueling. If we too are light physical vehicles, who eat high octane fuel, instead of low octane fuel, we'll also find ourselves moving a lot lighter, further, and faster.

Proper Rest

One cannot be successful in anything with constant fatigue and restlessness. Going to bed late and getting up early is a recipe for fatigue and disease, resulting from the lack of immunity repair. Your body is able to regenerate and heal itself through proper rest. Lack of good rest affects the brain and many other organs of the body.

There are several levels of sleep. Deep sleep is the most important level for benefiting the body. Deep sleep doesn't begin until approximately the fourth to fifth hour of undisturbed sleep. The more hours that your body has to sleep deeply, the more rejuvenated and healthy you will become. Unfortunately, our sleep routines prohibit us from getting ample deep sleep. Sad to say, some never reach this level of sleep. I encourage you to protect your health and live better through receiving proper rest.

> *Deep sleep doesn't begin until approximately the fourth to fifth hour of undisturbed sleep.*

Hydration

The human body is made of approximately 60-70% water. Everything in your body is made with some water content. Even your bones are made of 20% water. Without proper amounts of water, you are starving your body of the right to exist. The brain is made of approximately 85% water. In terms of enjoyable existence, the brain is the most important organ you have. It is the only thing that science cannot substitute. Since the brain is the most important and vital organ of the body and requires 85% of its mass to be water, then you see how important water is.

Allow me to address a myth. Soda, wine, milk, juice etc are not viable substitutes for good clean water. On average, healthy organs require a daily amount of water equivalent to half your body's weight - but in ounces. So, if you're 150 pounds in weight, then you would need 75 ounces of water each day. We've heard that a good amount of water is 8 (8-ounce) glasses of water or 64 ounces. While that rule of thumb is a good rule for some, it is only perfect for those weighing approximately 130 pounds. Therefore, in order for you to achieve the proper amount of water, nearly everything you drink each day should be water. Do your body a favor; give it life. It's Time!

> *....nearly everything you drink each day should be water.*

Creative Exercise

Our bodies are designed to move. As a soldier in the U.S. Army, I was trained to drive a tractor-trailer. In my training, I learned that many heavy vehicles have diesel engines. With the price of fuel lately, we are accustomed to turning off the engine when idle. However, with a diesel engine, it's actually bad practice to turn off the engine, even when it's idling for several hours. The reason is because diesel engines use glow plugs instead of spark plugs as with gas engines. In other words, unlike the gas engine, which uses the spark of fire to burn fuel, the diesel engine uses the heat of the glow plug to burn fuel. For maximum performance, the diesel engine must continue to operate in order for the plugs to remain hot enough to burn well. In other words, the hotter the glow plugs remain, the more easily the diesel engine can burn fuel. The more the diesel engine operates uninterrupted, the better it seems to perform. As you can imagine with that concept, the diesel engine is innately built for constant, heavy, and commercial use. In fact, a million miles is not unusual for the diesel engine unlike a gasoline engine, which operates approximately 300,000 miles before needing an overhaul.

One of the most effective ways to burn fat and carbohydrates is by walking.

The point of this information is this. Our physical bodies, made by God, were designed to operate for maximum use. Though we often seek ways to use our bodies as little as possible, we're actually hindering the performance and longevity of our organs, including the brain, when we minimize physical activity. The more our physical engines are in operation, the better we perform. A body in motion stays in motion, according to Newton's Law of Motion.

Pbs.org states that the heart will beat approximately 2.5 billion times in an average lifetime, pumping as many as 42 million gallons of blood. Your body was designed by God to perform at a high rate of intensity. You are indeed reverently and marvelously made, according to Psalm 139.

The less we use our bodies, the worse they will perform.

The less we use our bodies, the worse they will perform. Our bodies are not like gas engines, which work better as we use them as little as possible. Our bodies are like diesel engines. If we don't keep them active and running, we may incur complications brought on by inactivity. This includes obesity, heart disease, diabetes and many other things.

Some may ask, how do we bring on diseases from inactivity? While I am not a physician, please confirm the following statements with your doctor, as I have. The answer to the question is simply this. Whatever we eat that is not used by the body will be stored in our bodies, usually in the fat cells of our bodies. Excessive carbohydrates, protein and fat are all stored as fat, if not used. As with most things that we store too long, if they are warehoused for longer than the intended shelf life, they tend to create other challenges. From free radical cells to extended colon storage to unused fat to cholesterol, anything stored too long in the body becomes a health risk. In essence, we can become walking warehouses filled with hazardous material. I'm sure you don't want that for yourself and neither do I.

Instead of being warehouses, let us see ourselves as convenience stores – mini-marts, where we take in minimal supplies more often, while quickly using or completely burning what we eat. The more you take in, the more storage space you require and the more physical energy required to burn these calories.

In order to effectively burn these calories in storage, you must regularly schedule calorie-burning sessions – physical exercise. The more storage you have, the harder you'll have to work to get rid your storage size. But, on the bright side, there are many creative and fun methods that we can use to burn the excess storage in our bodies.

One of the most effective ways to burn calories is by walking. You can never walk too much. Running is a good exercise for athletes who are competing. However, running is not the best exercise for everyday people like you and me because of the harsh pounding upon the knees. Knee replacements are not something to look forward to. Vigorous walking and swimming are absolutely the most efficient and effective forms of exercise for the human body.

Find a way to make walking fun. Walking is the number one reason that I golf. Instead of using the golf cart to find my lost golf balls, I use my legs. You too can find new and creative reasons to use your legs, arms and muscles. In the end, you'll be glad you did.

Master Key # 5
Establish the Pillar of Faith

The term "faith" is to place confidence or trust in a thing, person, or deity. There are many deities and philosophies today, which attempt to explain the existence of man and the creation of the world. While being a philosophy and religion major in undergraduate school, I studied many religions, to include Christianity, Islam, Judaism, Sikhism, Buddhism, Hindu, Shintoism, Scientology, and Mormonism - just to name a few. I can honestly say that many of these religions have very good and positive belief systems. Many of them have very noble sets of moral teachings that share great commonality with each other.

In other words, I developed an appreciation for various faiths because of the good nature, sense of peace, and personal disciplines that they encourage. However, I have found only one faith that placed a well-balanced explanation of how things came into being - the creation of the universe. I have found only one faith that offered a set of morals that were noble, perfect, and yet seamless with our history, and could be proven with archaeology and science. I have found but one faith, which aligns its stories and foretelling of coming world events with our actual current events. This philosophy of faith outlines a clear thread between the existence of humanity and the existence of God.

This religion that I found to be true is substantiated through many followers who declare to have had encounters with the supernatural and divine interventions here in the natural realm. These divine encounters include innumerable medical reports of miracles and reports of life on the other side of death. Through my intense search of the faiths, I have found one clear seam with nature, the universe, man, and deity in the God of the Holy Bible.

The God of Abraham, Isaac, Jacob, Moses, Joseph, David, Solomon, and Elijah is the only true and living God, in my opinion. The Heavenly Father of Jesus Christ, the sacrificed ransom for the ills of mankind is the only true God.

The term "Christ" means the anointed of God, the Father. He is The Chosen One, the Divine Son of God, through Immaculate Conception, and born of a Jewish woman named Mary, Jesus Christ is our access to God - The Father of all things natural and spiritual. This child born of an earthly mother and Heavenly Father was the Moshiach, the Messiah sent by God, as the fee of atonement for mankind's breached relationship with God. From the beginning, man has been rebellious against The Father's instructions. This resulted in dissonance from God – a separation – a gap between the mistakes of mankind and the perfect intentions of God, the author of the universe. Mankind was required to pay penalties for the disobedience and dissonance against God's plan and instructions. Why the penalty? Without a penalty, mankind would repeatedly make the mistakes over and over again, as with any ordinance.

But, get this: you and I were not required to pay our own penalty for violating God's instructions. Because of the passionate love of God for us, Jesus, the Son and Messiah of the Father, paid the penalty for our reconnection back to God with his very life. Through a physical beating, crucifixion, and humiliation, Jesus took the penalty for all of us and became our bridge back to the Father of the Universe. Jesus redeemed and repurchased disobedient mankind, through the sacrifice of his own life and blood on a Cross, made by Roman soldiers over 2,000 years ago.

After a documented life and death in the journals of reputable historians such as Josephus, a reputable Jewish historian, Jesus who was dead and buried could not be found in his tomb. It is reported in the annals of history that angelic beings were left at the scene to report that Jesus was again alive and seated beside his Father in the Heavens, after paying a dear price to reconcile mankind back to God. Because of Jesus' obedience to death on the cross of crucifixion, Jesus was rewarded and raised from the burial tomb by his divine Father in order to prove his deity and connection with The Father of the Universe. In other words, Jesus' obedience replaced our disobedience and through his resurrection from the dead became our reason to believe in Jesus Christ, as the representative for God the Father of All.

Well, how can this be proven? According to history, Jesus came back to show himself to his followers and many others, who reported that they, not only saw Jesus alive after his death, but not sure Jesus was touched and talked to the risen Jesus, who later ascended back to his Father in heaven. Jesus, according to the testimonies of witnesses now resides in Heaven and sits on the right hand of the throne of his Father.

The most fascinating thing about all of this is that Jesus' birth was predicted hundreds of years in advance. Forecasters of God called prophets reported in writing that the divine Son of God would be sent to the earth hundreds of years before God actually sent Jesus to earth through Mary, his natural mother.

Jesus said, while on earth, that he is going to be sent to earth by his Father a SECOND TIME – possibly in our lifetime to escort the faithful back to God the Father. As recorded by reporters and witnesses in the Holy Scriptures, Jesus himself said that he was returning to earth to take his followers (believers) back to heaven with him. I, personally, believe that if Jesus returns today, my faith and personal lifestyle would be aligned in such as way that I could return with him. Not because of my own righteousness would I return with Jesus, but because of my faith and obedience to Jesus Christ would I return with Him. **Jesus paid my fee for all past, current and future disobedience and now I obey Jesus instructions in return**.

I have accepted Jesus Christ, the Holy Spirit and the Heavenly Father as my one unified God. These three presentations of God operate as one single unit, which require my loyalty, love, honor and service to his sovereignty and limitless power and wisdom. In addition, the morals and values found in the teachings of the Bible yield an incredible benefit not only to me, but everyone around me. **It's Time** to fully establish your faith in Jesus Christ.

Interested in having a successful after-life?

5 Steps to Making Peace with God.

1. Believe that Jesus Christ is the divine Son of God. Study the Holy Bible for yourself or ask a bible teacher to assist you.
2. Believe in your heart that Jesus came to earth and returned to heaven, after being crucified – losing his blood and natural life, as a sacrifice to His Father for all of our ignorance and disobedience against the Creator. Believe that Jesus was raised from the dead by God his Heavenly Father after three days of physical burial.
3. Announce your belief in this faith aloud before a witness and join a Christian church that teaches the Holy Bible regularly.
4. Continue to live your life by the teachings of Jesus Christ, found in the Holy Bible. I recommend the New Revised Standard Version of the Holy Bible. After studying the original languages of the bible in an academic setting, this version is very accurate and has my full confidence. I suggest the English Standard Version for the Old Testament.
5. Tell someone else of your experience and invite them to be prepared for Jesus' return.

The term "faith" is to place a blind belief or trust in a person, thing, or deity. There are many deities, which require pure faith, having no physical artifacts, no reports of actual divine presence, and no real connections between God and humanity. The belief in the Holy Bible, in my opinion, provides more hardcore evidence and reasons to believe than any other religion that I've studied. My recommendation for life-long faith, is the belief in Jesus Christ, God's chosen redeemer and connector with mankind. In this section of the book, I want to illuminate God's order for man from the beginning of creation to today's implementation of faith.

"Theos" is a Greek term for God. Theology is the study of God. Anthropology is the study of man. A successful life and after-life are impossible to achieve without a study of God's plan for man. Using this master key, we will study the relationship of God and Man. I am honored to be your guide inside this study of God, my favorite subject.

> *A successful life and after-life are impossible to achieve without faith in God.*

FAITH IS A RAINBOW

Faith is a rock when values become slippery.
Faith is a compass when truth becomes trickery.

Faith is a refuge that removes all fret.
Faith is an action that removes future regret.

Faith is a boundary, protecting you from harm.
Faith is a harvest, protecting your financial farm.

Faith is a rainbow after a bit of adversity,
because rainbows end storms and begin possibility.

- Joe McDaniel

LIFE LESSON 19
Follow God's Order for Humanity

In the beginning, God placed all things in **order**. Today, that order continues to be sure and prescribed for us. God's order for man is a perpetual state of structure, calculated movement, and Godly actions, which allow us to maintain healthy lives and spiritual relationships with Him and each other. This structure and ordained movement are laid out in the first book of the Bible – Genesis. The first thirteen verses of the book of Genesis lists some of the most important events in the history of the universe. God begins the order of man by creating a habitat for man. We will find that this **habitat for man consisted of three things**: the sun, the body, and the garden.

- The sun indicates God's likeness and ordained nature for man, which is that of **light**.
- The body indicates the **form** of our physical image, which is to always be in the image of God.
- The garden indicates a place of **seed** and provision, which are provided for the daily nurturing and abundance for man.

As we take a close look at the first few verses of Genesis, we get a better idea of how God uses light of the son, form from God's image and the seed of the garden, to produce a lifestyle fit for his royal children, man and woman. Light, Form and Seed is the topic of our lesson. Let us look at Genesis 1 very carefully.

> *1In the beginning, God created the heavens and the earth. 2The earth was without form and void, and darkness was over the face of the deep. And the Spirit of God was hovering over the face of the waters.*
>
> *3And God said, "Let there be light," and there was light. 4 And God saw that the light was good. And God separated the light from the darkness. 5 God called the light Day, and the darkness he called Night. And there was evening and there was morning, the first day.*
>
> *6And God said, "Let there be an expanse in the midst of the waters, and let it separate the waters from the waters." 7And God made the expanse and separated the waters that were under the expanse from the waters that were above the expanse. And it was so. 8And God called the expanse Heaven. And there was evening and there was morning, the second day.*
>
> *9And God said, "Let the waters under the heavens be gathered together into one place, and let the dry land appear." And it was so. 10God called the dry land Earth, and the waters that were gathered together he called Seas. And God saw that it was good.*

11And God said, "Let the earth sprout vegetation, plants yielding seed, and fruit trees bearing fruit in which is their seed, each according to its kind, on the earth." And it was so. 12The earth brought forth vegetation, plants yielding seed according to their own kinds, and trees bearing fruit in which is their seed, each according to its kind. And God saw that it was good. 13And there was evening and there was morning, the third day.

The Light

In verse three, God says "Let there be light, and there was light." And, he called the light good. Light is a good thing to God and is a good thing for man. God never said, let there be darkness. Darkness was perpetual in the beginning. It was a constant state of barrenness and blindness, as there was absolutely no light on the earth, no life, no vegetation – nothing. Everything was void, empty, and very very dark. God never called darkness good. He only called light good. God never intended for man to live in this deep state of darkness, so he created light for man.

Unfortunately, we may find pockets of darkness in our lives, or areas where there is a grip of dark struggles in critical areas where we live. These pockets of darkness may be found in a failing marriage, financial struggle, or physical sickness. Know that God never intended for man to constantly dwell in any state of darkness, bareness, unfruitfulness or fear, but in a state of light and productivity.

> *...God never intended for man to constantly dwell in any state of darkness, but in a state of light.*

In verse 4 of Genesis 1, God separated the light from the darkness. During this brief moment in the early state of the universe, light and darkness dwelled together. The two must have been intermingled somehow. This would have been a very unusual sight at that time, though not so unusual in society today. But, God divided or separated light from darkness for a distinct reason. He did not want mankind to live in darkness nor in an intermingled state of mixed darkness and mixed light, but rather periods where we cycle through or merely pass through a phase of darkness and then a phase of light - or night and day.

> *God is not interested at all in our lifestyle of mixed godliness with ungodliness.*

From a spiritual standpoint, God is not interested at all in our lifestyle of mixed godliness with ungodliness. He is looking for distinct delineation of light from darkness. **Remember, God loves light not darkness.** Usually, anything heavily associated with utter darkness or night is of an evil or ungodly nature.

In verse 5 of Genesis 1, "He called the light day, and the darkness he called night. God's intent was never to totally remove man from darkness, but to allow darkness to remain as a separated cycle, well in reach for man. Or better stated, God wanted to always allow light to be a hope in reach, by way of a constant bridge of time, as a reminder that light is possible. In a spiritual sense, man will dwell with the darkness of the world and the darkness of life, but these periods of temptations, struggle, stumble, darkness are only cycles through which man must pass. In other words, God called periods of darkness, that we regularly experience, "night". Night is a cycle that we, God's children, will experience by a natural and spiritual clock. There will be periods of vulnerability, but we must rest in our night seasons, knowing that God will protect us from the evil and temptation, as we solicit his protection through prayer.

Total darkness is a solid state considerably different from periodic darkness. Darkness is a state of sin and ungodly habitat.

We are NOT people of the dark. Jesus calls us Children of the light.

Jesus put it in these words in John 12:35-36,

> [35] *Jesus said to them, 'The light is with you for a little longer. Walk while you have the light, so that the darkness may not overtake you. If you walk in the darkness, you do not know where you are going.* [36] *While you have the light, believe in the light, so that you may become children of light.'*

There is an appreciation that man will have for light after experiencing total darkness. In darkness, it is impossible to see without the aid of some form of light or someone carrying light for you. It is difficult to work or do anything productive without the wisdom of light. There is only one light that will aid man in a situation of total darkness. Jesus Christ. Just before performing a miracle, Jesus explains in John 9:3-5,

> [3] *Jesus answered, 'Neither this man nor his parents sinned; he was born blind so that God's works might be revealed in him.* [4] *We must work the works of him who sent me while it is day; night is coming when no one can work.* [5] *As long as I am in the world, I am the light of the world.'*

Once again, there is a temporary state of darkness, which is spiritually equivalent to blindness, being lost or disoriented. There is also the much more permanent apocalyptic state of abandoned darkness that Jesus talked about when no one will be able to work, because of the eternal removal of light from our world. But Jesus puts distance between that permanent state and our current state by saying, "As long as I am in the world, I am the light of the world." Allow me to make these words very clear. **Jesus is the light of the world!** While we have Jesus and His followers, spiritually, as the light of the world, we don't have to live in darkness or be eternally lost in darkness.

I believe that God allows night and day cycles to help us understand the dependence that we should have for the light of Jesus Christ. Allow me to repeat an earlier statement; there is an appreciation that man has for light after experiencing darkness. We can appreciate working in light, after trying to perform any simple task in complete darkness. But since God did not allow man to experience this perpetual state of darkness in the beginning of creation, we have no concept of perpetual darkness, bareness or hell, only

> *...God allows night and day to help us understand the dependence we should have for the light of Jesus Christ.*

the temporary cycles of night and day. But once again, Jesus said, there is coming a much longer period of spiritual night, when no man will be able to work. We must work now, while it is day. This is the opportunity that we have right now to labor as children of God, children of the Light.

I believe that this state of darkness that Jesus refers to when no man can work is simultaneous spiritual death and natural death. There is a season when we are alive, given a candle of life, and able to work while we are alive. Being asleep versus awake is a natural model of this spiritual concept. At night, we sleep; in daylight, we're hopefully awake. The bible discusses the difference between sleep and death. Rev. 14:13

> *13 And I heard a voice from heaven saying, 'Write this: Blessed are the dead who from now on die in the Lord.' 'Yes,' says the Spirit, 'they will rest from their labours, for their deeds follow them.*

Death is a time when man is not allowed to do any further spiritual or natural preparation on the earth. As such, this is a period of spiritual resting or natural death, before the great judgment of God. Rev. 14:11-15

> *11 Then I saw a great white throne and the one who sat on it; the earth and the heaven fled from his presence, and no place was found for them. [12]And I saw the dead, great and small, standing before the throne, and books were opened. Also another book was opened, the book of life. And the dead were judged according to their works, as recorded in the books. [13]And the sea gave up the dead that were in it, Death and Hades gave up the dead that were in them, and all were judged according to what they had done. [14]Then Death and Hades were thrown into the lake of fire. This is the second death, the lake of fire; [15]and anyone whose name was not found written in the book of life was thrown into the lake of fire.*

There is yet another state that is slightly different. Jesus calls it sleep. It is when you give the signs of natural death, but are not finished with work on Earth. Jesus may call this temporary state of natural death a state of sleep, where unlike death, you can be awakened. Matthew 9:24-25

> *[24]he said, 'Go away; for the girl is not dead but sleeping.' And they laughed at him. [25]But when the crowd had been put outside, he went in and took her by the hand, and the girl got up.*

With regard to spiritual sleep versus permanent death, Jesus instructs us as follows, in the parable of the ten virgins. Mathew 25:1-13

> *Then the kingdom of heaven will be like this. Ten bridesmaids* took their lamps and went to meet the bridegroom. [2]Five of them were foolish, and five were wise. [3]When the foolish took their lamps, they took no oil with them; [4]but the wise took flasks of oil with their lamps. [5]As the bridegroom was delayed, all of them became drowsy and slept. [6]But at midnight there was a shout, "Look! Here is the bridegroom! Come out to meet him."*
> *[7]Then all those bridesmaids got up and trimmed their lamps. [8]The foolish said to the wise, "Give us some of your oil, for our lamps are going out." [9]But the wise replied, "No! there will not be enough for you and*

for us; you had better go to the dealers and buy some for yourselves." [10]*And while they went to buy it, the bridegroom came, and those who were ready went with him into the wedding banquet; and the door was shut.* [11]*Later the other bridesmaids came also, saying, "Lord, lord, open to us."* [12]*But he replied, "Truly I tell you, I do not know you."* [13]*Keep awake therefore, for you know neither the day nor the hour.*

Jesus tells us to stay awake. Even as we cycle through temporary states of darkness, Jesus tells us to keep awake. Just as night comes, darkness comes upon us, as well as sleep and slumber. When darkness comes over us, we may feel an inclination to succumb to spiritual sleep, slumber, disobedience, and riotous living. It is risky to sleep in spiritual darkness, knowing that Jesus may come or worse death while in this dark state. In order to survive the temptation to succumb to spiritual sleep and darkness, we must remain awake and alert with the light that comes from the oil of God's spirit through Jesus Christ. There is a period that God calls midnight (no man knows the exact time) when the bridegroom will return to rescue us from the coming more permanent state of darkness that Jesus talks about in John 12:35.

God intended for us to encounter night and dark. However, he wants us to resist darkness and spiritual sleep.

In order for us to become mature Christians and be successful in the things of life and Godliness, we must build our resistance to darkness.

We cannot forget that God called us to be in the world, but not of the world. In John 17:14-19, Jesus prays to the Heavenly Father:

[14]*I have given them your word, and the world has hated them because they do not belong to the world, just as I do not belong to the world.* [15]*I am not asking you to take them out of the world, but I ask you to protect them from the evil one.* [16]*They do not belong to the world, just as I do not belong to the world.* [17]*Sanctify them in the truth; your word is truth.* [18]*As you have sent me into the world, so I have sent them into the world.* [19]*And for their sakes I sanctify myself, so that they also may be sanctified in truth.*

Jesus says that though we do not belong to the world of darkness, we are required to reside in the world, as the Father and the sanctification process protect us from the evil one. The root word "sanctify" in the Greek denotes being set-apart from ungodly or dark things, ungodly thinking and ungodly lifestyles. Jesus says that we are to sanctify ourselves through His word – or in other words practicing the teachings and principles of the Holy Bible.

Darkness is all around, but we are to be separated from darkness only by the light of the world, Jesus Christ. By resisting darkness and the Evil One, we can assume that we will not fall asleep.

God did not intend for us to participate in acts of the world's darkness, but rather as children of light, infiltrate the world, while not becoming partakers, partners, or joined to the world. The Apostle

Paul asked the church at Corinth the following question: What fellowship has light with darkness? Specifically, he says it this way in 2 Corinthians 6:14-18:

> [14]*Do not be mismatched with unbelievers. For what partnership is there between righteousness and lawlessness? Or what fellowship is there between light and darkness?* [15]*What agreement does Christ have with Belial? Or what does a believer share with an unbeliever?* [16]*What agreement has the temple of God with idols? For we are the temple of the living God; as God said, 'I will live in them and walk among them, and I will be their God, and they shall be my people.* [17] *Therefore come out from them, and be separate from them, says the Lord, and touch nothing unclean; then I will welcome you,* [18]*and I will be your father, and you shall be my sons and daughters, says the Lord Almighty.'*

God said, "Let there be light". Many centuries later, Jesus, the light of the world appeared on the earth in the midst of spiritual darkness. God saw that light and said that it was good. Consider the following passage from John 3:16-21.

> *'For God so loved the world that he gave his only Son, so that everyone who believes in him may not perish but may have eternal life.*
> *Indeed, God did not send the Son into the world to condemn the world, but in order that the world might be saved through him. Those who believe in him are not condemned; but those who do not believe are condemned already, because they have not believed in the name of the only Son of God. And this is the judgment, that the light has come into the world, and people loved darkness rather than light because their deeds were evil. For all who do evil hate the light and do not come to the light, so that their deeds may not be exposed. But those who do what is true come to the light, so that it may be clearly seen that their deeds have been done in God.'*

John 8:12 further adds to the discussion.

> *Again Jesus spoke to them, saying, 'I am the light of the world. Whoever follows me will never walk in darkness but will have the light of life.*

Then God caused a separation of that light. Paul further explains this concept of light, darkness, and separation in the 5th chapter of Ephesians.

> *6 Let no one deceive you with empty words, for because of these things the wrath of God comes on those who are disobedient.* [7]*Therefore do not be associated with them.* [8]*For once you were darkness, but now in the Lord you are light. Live as children of light—*[9]*for the fruit of the light is found in all that is good and right and true.* [10]*Try to find out what is pleasing to the Lord.* [11]*Take no part in the unfruitful works of darkness, but instead expose them.* [12]*For it is shameful even to mention what such people do secretly;* [13]*but everything exposed by the light becomes visible,* [14]*for everything that becomes visible is light. Therefore it says, 'Sleeper, awake! Rise from the dead, and Christ will shine on you.'*

In the first five verses of Ephesians chapter 5, Paul exposes darkness and provides a clear connection between the light of the world and His children of light, by saying, "but now in the Lord you are light." When God said in Genesis, let there be light and Jesus, the light of the world later appeared on the earth, know that we "in the Lord" are also a part of that light – children of light. Paul echoes and illuminates God's intentional separation from light and darkness, just as was ordered by God in the beginning. Note how Paul descriptively identifies the behavior of darkness from that of the light of God. Ephesians 5:1-5

> [1] *Therefore be imitators of God, as beloved children,* [2] *and live in love, as Christ loved us* and gave himself up for us, a fragrant offering and sacrifice to God.*
> *3 But fornication and impurity of any kind, or greed, must not even be mentioned among you, as is proper among saints.* [4] *Entirely out of place is obscene, silly, and vulgar talk; but instead, let there be thanksgiving.* [5] *Be sure of this, that no fornicator or impure person, or one who is greedy (that is, an idolater), has any inheritance in the kingdom of Christ and of God.*

Light was the first item of infrastructure for the habitat of man that God spoke into existence. Light followed the first "Let there be". Light was the only agenda item for God on the first day of creation.

You'll notice that the first thing that God does before he wakes us every morning is turn on the lights for us. With sunrise, Mother Nature's lights are turned on so brightly, that we can sometimes avoid the use of man-made light. Nevertheless, we too, like God must engage our spiritual light switch.

The spiritual parallel is that you must also turn on your spiritual light. In other words, though you naturally awake in a bit of a slumber every morning, your spiritual lights must also be turned on. First thing in the morning, you must illuminate your spiritual day in such a way that you are able to clearly see and understand God's spiritual direction for you. As there is natural light turned on by God each morning, there is also an enabling of spiritual sight through the inner illuminations that you receive through prayer and scriptural devotion. Prov. 20:27 says,

> *God uses every individual's own inner spirit as His own divine lamp. It is the conscience of man.*

"The spirit of man is the lamp of the Lord, searching all his innermost parts."

God uses every individual's own inner spirit as His divine lamp. It is the conscience of man. God uses man's own personal spirit as His light to help guide man. I believe that every man and woman who is alive has enough inner light to find their way to God, if they only choose to. Light, by design, is usually in reach to mankind, if he or she desires more light. The very spirit of man, which was initially breathed by God, provides illuminations, even understanding for the way that you should take in every moment and every situation. Man's inner light is his conscience, which can naturally decipher right from wrong. It is vitally important that we be guided by our inner spirits – our peace. The notion of light is a key element in understanding faith in your creator.

After creating light the second item on God's mind was form and structure of creation.

The Form

The second verse of Genesis 1 (the first chapter) says, "the earth was without form". To be without form is to be without shape or order. The first point of infrastructure that God set in place was light and the second point of infrastructure was form. At the rudimentary stages of order, everything must take on form or shape or basic order. We must understand that at the beginning of the world, everything was dark, void, empty, without any order and without any shape. It may be difficult to imagine the world in this state of chaos, but it also shows the power and glory of God to be able create a habitat for man out of complete chaos. By the way, if your life feels like this state of chaos, please know that our God specializes in create beauty out of chaos.

Let's further attempt to imagine what the cosmos was like in the beginning. There are many things that do not have shape or form. For example, water, wind, and gases are items that do not have any particular form or shape. Dirt is another item that does not have form. The shapelessness of elements, matter, and gases were the environment that God encountered before the earth was formed.

In order to create a habitable breathable home for man, God needed to carefully and creatively form the planet Earth for man to live. Remember, there was no Earth in the beginning, until, "God created the Heaven and the Earth". There was no heaven until God created it. And, he carefully created it all with the power of his spoken word.

When we think of the spoken words of God, we must be mindful that the word of the Father is a spiritual force that materializes and becomes whatever God, the Father, speaks. According to John 1:1, Jesus Christ is named the "word" of the Father, as powerful words are the actual force and agent of all of creation. In the beginning, all things were made by God's words. So then, it follows that all things spoken in creation were created by the Father's key agent and son, Jesus Christ – the powerful word of God, our Father.

Oftentimes, it may be challenging to understand how the Son of God is one with God, but yet different from God, the Father. It was challenging for me for many years. In humanity, the male offspring of a parent is known as a son. Likewise, to the Father of the Universe, his offspring is considered his actual word - the Word of the Father, which materializes and becomes or forms whatever He speaks. This is a mysterious concept to grasp, but very real, as we exist everyday as a result of the powerful word (offspring) of God – which the Father has named Jesus Christ. Consider the following passage from John chapter 1:1-14.

In the beginning was the Word, and the Word was with God, and the Word was God. [2]He was in the beginning with God. [3]All things came into being through him, and without him not one thing came into being. What has come into being [4]in him was life, and the life was the light of all people. [5]The light shines in the darkness, and the darkness did not overcome it. 6 There was a man sent from God, whose name was John. [7]He came as a witness to testify to the light, so that all might believe through him. [8]He himself was not the light, but he came to testify to the light. [9]The true light, which enlightens everyone, was coming into the world. 10 He was in the world, and the world came into being through him; yet the world did not know him. [11]He came to what was his own, and his own people did not accept him. [12]But to all who received him, who believed in his name, he gave power to become children of God, [13]who were born, not of blood or of the will of the flesh or of the will of man, but of God. 14 And the Word became flesh and lived among us, and we have seen his glory, the glory as of a father's only son, full of grace and truth.

I should also note that this creative force in creation, known as the Word of God continues today to hold the universe together as a constant reminder of the power of God's word still in existence. Consider the following passage from Hebrews 1:2-3.

²but in these last days he has spoken to us by a Son, whom he appointed heir of all things, through whom he also created the worlds. ³He is the reflection of God's glory and the exact imprint of God's very being, and he sustains all things by his powerful word.

Having set a brief foundation for how Jesus participated in Creation with the Father, Let's continue with the story of how God, the Father, formed all things through the power of his word. On the second day, in the verses of Genesis between 6 and 8 God formed the heavens, by speaking the following words:

6 And God said, "Let there be an expanse in the midst of the waters, and let it separate the waters from the waters." 7 And God made the expanse and separated the waters that were under the expanse from the waters that were above the expanse. And it was so. 8 And God called the expanse Heaven. And there was evening and there was morning, the second day.

The original Hebrew term for expanse is "עִיקָר" or "raqia". It denotes a spread out area or spread out opening. It is better known to us as the upward space above the earth. It is the sky, outer space, or the heavens. When we imagine God before there was an earth, we need to see Him more clearly as one who existed in the time of history before there was a heaven or an earth. During this early time of cosmic history, there were only gases, air, matter, natural elements and water. And, all of this matter, gas, and water were all intermingled to create a cosmic mess. There was no clear opening of space for which birds or planes could fly. It must have been a conglomeration of total disorder, flying debris and matter, such that man could not habitat. So then, after creating light, God needed to develop heaven, clean air and space by first creating a free and clear open area.

Again, we call this open area the sky; the ESV Bible calls this area an expanse. Before a baby is born, the only world that the baby knows is a world of water, fluid, and the minerals and chemicals that exist all around the baby in the womb; creation in the beginning was in a similar womb of water and debris. According to the Bible in verses 6-8 of Genesis 1, the pre-birth state of the cosmos, heaven, and certainly earth was water - a womb of water.

If there is an opening called outer space, which separates the waters above outer space from the waters below outer space, then it follows that water still remains above outer space. (Gen. 1:6-10). I suppose no satellite would be able to travel far enough to verify this, as it would be, perhaps trillions of light years away. This is all very fascinating to me. NASA confirms that outer space is so large that it would take years and years to reach certain parts of outer space - even traveling at the speed of light, if that constant speed of travel were ever possible.

It is very interesting how God formed this vast opening, called heaven. Please bear in mind that according to Genesis 1:1, God created the heavens, plural, not just Heaven. Science, cosmology, and astrology agree that the heavens are multi-dimensional. In other words, planet earth is but a grain of sand on a continental beach compared to the full size and capacity of the heavens.

Allow me to detail the size of this expanse or the heavens that God created. Our sun and earth is a part of the galaxy called "the Milky Way", which includes one hundred thousand million other stars. (in other words, at least 100,000 x 1,000,000 stars are in our galaxy). A number this large is well into the trillions. In other words, there are more than a trillion stars the size of earth in our galaxy, far too many to count. It would be challenging for a bank to count a trillion dollars, let alone a trillion stars, all spread out over space.

Some of these stars are much larger than our Sun, if that gives you a better idea of the size and space we are discussing. Remember, trillions of stars and suns are in our one galaxy alone – the Milky Way. But, here's what's even more fascinating.

There are millions and millions of other galaxies, which include their own groupings of trillions of stars and suns. When we include every galaxy that God spoke into existence, we then realize that we are talking about an opening or expanse, the size of which is impossible for our delicate little minds to imagine. Modeling the depth, breath, and width of a galaxy is impossible, but the thought of modeling the size of a trillion other galaxies is totally beyond human comprehension. When God said, "let there be light", there was light!

No scientist or astronaut can possibly travel far enough to ever see the ends of space – ever, at least not in human form or life-span. But, for the sake of this writing, somewhere on the top and bottom sides of this extremely vast expanse of space and light, is possibly water, according to my interpretation of the scripture.

God took one day to create the stars, moon, and sun; God took a day to create space, and God took a third day to create the earth in great detail. Please keep in mind that there is still much debate about whether our 24-hour day and God's day is the exact same. It wasn't until the fourth day, or verse 14 of Genesis one, that God created the full magnitude of all the stars in space, but it's all very incredible when we talk about God bringing form and order to the universe. Let us examine this forming process a little closer.

> *To think of what God actually did to create a habitat for man is extremely humbling.*

To think of what God actually did to create a habitat for man is extremely humbling. God created many things by His Word and by His Spirit. Remember, before God ever spoke anything, His spirit, the Spirit of God, first hovered over what is called the "face of the deep" and the "face of the waters". In light of the size and magnitude of everything appearing in the midst of God before the creation, it was all referred to as "the deep". It was this great deep eternity of darkness and enormous volume of water that was the object of a day's work for our amazing God and Creator. The Spirit of God hovered over this great deep mass, preparing to bring form, separation, and order to all of it. Genesis 1:6 once more,

6 And God said, "Let there be an expanse in the midst of the waters, and let it separate the waters from the waters." 7 And God made the expanse and separated the waters that were under the expanse from the waters that were above the expanse. And it was so. 8 And God called the expanse Heaven. And there was evening and there was morning, the second day.

Now that Heaven had been formed, God needed to form the earth. As the spirit of God was still hovering over the great deep, God speaks again on the third day.

9 And God said, "Let the waters under the heavens be gathered together into one place, and let the dry land appear." And it was so. 10 God called the dry land Earth, and the waters that were gathered together he called Seas. And God saw that it was good.

There "are" waters above the heavens, and there "were" waters under the heavens, which covered all land, and perhaps planets. God commanded all of the waters under the expanse of space to be gathered into one place, so that "dry" land could appear, creating Earth made of both land and water. Here are the powerful words of God in affect – powerful enough to order the waters in outer space and command them to be confined to one area. This was the process by which God gave form to the heavens and the earth. We don't know exactly how God formed the earth, but the first verse of Genesis says that the earth was without form initially and now, of course, the earth has clear form.

In a latter instance of creation, God formed man. In verse 7, of Genesis chapter 2, the Bible says that, *"the Lord God formed man of the dust of the ground, and breathed into his nostrils the breath of life, and man became a living soul." – King James Version*

Air has no form; water has no form. These items only take on form when placed in a container. For example, a balloon or a ball takes on its proper form when it is filled with air; a sand bag takes on form when it is filled with formless sand. Man (made of dust) took on form when God breathed His spirit, His pneuma, His life into man. God's spirit is also His own image (John 4:24).

When the air is taken from a balloon, it loses its complete form. Likewise, when the spirit or breath of a man is taken, he or she dies and slowly loses the bodily form as reflected by the image of God's breath, which inhabited it. As a result, the spiritless body eventually returns to dust again – void and without form. Dust has no form, unless God breaths spirit into it and gives it form. **The form, image and likeness of God is what man is to always envy.**

The spirit of God hovered upon the waters and began to bring form to the heavens and the earth. The spirit of God also moved inside man and man took on God's form and image. Wherever God's spirit is, there is form and order. Wherever God's Spirit is not present, there is chaos, disorder or a lack of form.

Where ever God's Spirit is, there is form and order. Where ever God's spirit is not present, there is chaos.

So then, God spoke on the 3rd day and created heaven or the expanse by His words. He also spoke and brought form to the earth. He formed man, by breathing His own spirit and image into dust and the dust became alive. Heaven and earth did not take form, until God's spirit hovered over it.

God desires to give you form – a new form. That form is Jesus Christ, through the Holy Spirit. In Galatians 4 and 19, Paul briefly mentions this concept to his followers.

19"My little children, for whom I am again in the pain of childbirth until Christ is formed in you

The forming is a spiritual process, whereby God, through his Holy Spirit, develops us into the nature of Christ, through the teachings of the Bible and the guidance of the Holy Spirit and spiritual leaders like Apostle Paul. God has exemplified this forming process of order through creation.

The Seed

Still on the 3rd day, God speaks a second time, now focused on preparing food for man.

> *11 And God said, "Let the earth sprout vegetation, plants yielding seed, and fruit trees bearing fruit in which is their seed, each according to its kind, on the earth." And it was so. 12 The earth brought forth vegetation, plants yielding seed according to their own kinds, and trees bearing fruit in which is their seed, each according to its kind. And God saw that it was good. 13 And there was evening and there was morning, the third day.*

Let's review. There are three things that are important to God and critical to the existence of man – Light, Form, and Seed.

> *There are three things that are important to God and critical to the existence of man – Light, Form, and Seed.*

The third phase of creation that was most important to God was the seed. The seed of an apple is inside the apple; the seed of man is inside the man. God gave man seed for perpetual provisions and regeneration. Only once did God plant vegetation. After he planted all vegetation with His Word, the seeds of vegetation continued to fall upon the ground to sprout perpetual growth. After creation, Adam never needed to "create" trees, crops, or vegetation again. Adam only needed to go out and replant the seed or take hold of the provisions that God had already provided. To build homes, timber was already provided because of seed, which reproduced itself. Heat, through firewood was already provided because of the seed of trees; man never needed to invent food because of the seed that God established; work and trade came into existence because of the seed of God. Plastic comes from seed, rubber comes from seed; fuel also comes from seed. God fully provided for man – abundantly through the concept of the seed, which reproduces itself on its own. What a thoughtful and caring Creator?

There is a system of provision that the creator set in order. Our heavenly Father demonstrated this system. We are to sow, plant, and invest for an expected return. God desired a plentiful crop of righteous children, so he planted a seed into the earth that would be buried three days before sprouting a return of righteous souls, who are today called Christians (after God's seed – Jesus, the Christ). That is the Gospel in a nutshell. Just as your Heavenly Father gets what he wants through a seed, he also expects us to acquire our desired provisions with seeds, ideas, investments of some thing in hopes of the return of something else.

> *We are to sow, plant and invest for an expected return.*

Jesus further discusses the seed more spiritually. In Luke 6, Jesus suggests that one action breeds a following and subsequent result.

37 Do not judge, and you will not be judged; do not condemn, and you will not be condemned. Forgive, and you will be forgiven; ³⁸give, and it will be given to you. A good measure, pressed down, shaken together, running over, will be put into your lap; for the measure you give will be the measure you get back.

Paul, the Apostle of Jesus Christ continued Jesus' teaching in Galatians 6:

7 Do not be deceived; God is not mocked, for you reap whatever you sow. ⁸If you sow to your own flesh, you will reap corruption from the flesh; but if you sow to the Spirit, you will reap eternal life from the Spirit. ⁹So let us not grow weary in doing what is right, for we will reap at harvest time, if we do not give up.

The principle of sowing applies not only to money (through investments) and provisions (through agriculture), and kindness (through) morality, but it applies to the entire natural and spiritual life. The blessing and provision system of God is very intentional. From the beginning of creation, God intended for man to depend upon Him and His laws for financial sustenance, through sowing natural and spiritual seeds of investments and charity, respectively. Consider 2 Cor. 9:

6 The point is this: the one who sows sparingly will also reap sparingly, and the one who sows bountifully will also reap bountifully. ⁷Each of you must give as you have made up your mind, not reluctantly or under compulsion, for God loves a cheerful giver. ⁸And God is able to provide you with every blessing in abundance, so that by always having enough of everything, you may share abundantly in every good work. ⁹As it is written, 'He scatters abroad, he gives to the poor; his righteousness endures forever.' ¹⁰He who supplies seed to the sower and bread for food will supply and multiply your seed for sowing and increase the harvest of your righteousness.* ¹¹You will be enriched in every way for your great generosity, which will produce thanksgiving to God through us; ¹²for the rendering of this ministry not only supplies the needs of the saints but also overflows with many thanksgivings to God. ¹³Through the testing of this ministry you glorify God by your obedience to the confession of the gospel of Christ and by the generosity of your sharing with them and with all others, ¹⁴while they long for you and pray for you because of the surpassing grace of God that he has given you. ¹⁵Thanks be to God for his indescribable gift!

God intended for you to live by literal bread and spiritual seed, which are also his very words planted in your heart. Consider Matt. 4:

> [4]*But he answered, 'It is written,*
> *"One does not live by bread alone,*
> *but by every word that comes from the mouth of God."'*

God's word is like seed. When we plant the Words of Jesus Christ, who is the seed, into our bodies of dust and earth, it brings forth growth and hefty returns to the Kingdom of God. In this passage, Jesus reveals that though man needs natural strength, which comes from natural bread, we also need to develop spiritual strength by planting seeds of God's Word in our lives. There are many divine interpretations of the seed that we need to understand.

Jesus himself was a seed. In John 12:24, Jesus says these words,

> *"Very truly, I tell you, unless a grain of wheat falls into the earth and dies, it remains just a single grain; but if it dies, it bears much fruit."*

Jesus knew that he himself was seed that the Father would plant in the grave of the earth for three days. Once Jesus was sprouted from the dead, the Father reaped a harvest of many souls, through Jesus' punishment, death and burial on our sinful behalf. Jesus is the Word of God, the seed of the Heavenly Father made flesh and planted into the earth. Likewise, we plant God's Word (according to John 1), Jesus Christ, into the soil of our lives that we too might bear and return much fruit to the Father. Jesus was the model of how we are to lay down our lives in seed form, so that someone else can be the Father's harvest and live and know the Heavenly Father in an eternal way. Consider Mathew 17:

> 5 *The apostles said to the Lord, 'Increase our faith!'* [6] *The Lord replied, 'If you had faith the size of a mustard seed, you could say to this mulberry tree, "Be uprooted and planted in the sea", and it would obey you.*

In this passage, Jesus explains the power of Faith in a parable. Parables must be interpreted oftentimes. Seeds are rarely used in its current state. Seeds must be planted, watered, developed and grown in order to reach its full potential. Remember, Jesus responded to the request or perhaps the question. How do we increase our faith?

It is important to understand that God expects us to operate and live life through small initiations of faith, which are often called seed faith. When the disciples asked about increasing their faith, Jesus talks about seed. In other words, starting small, where you are, but simultaneously seeing the ending and full potential of what could be is the goal of seed-like faith.

Although seed has a spiritual connotation today, it also has a very natural connotation. Consider Genesis 26:12, 13.

> *And Isaac sowed in that land and reaped in the same year a hundredfold. The Lord blessed him, 13 and the man became rich, and gained more and more until he became very wealthy.*

Here in this passage, Isaac sowed natural seed in the land. This means that he farmed the land and sowed seed in conjunction with his faith in God, which grew and produced a major crop. In this example, we see how the natural seed suddenly becomes supernatural or converts to spiritual seed, so to speak. Isaac reaped in the same year from his planting of seed a hundredfold. That's one-hundred new seeds for one. For example, one dollar became 100 dollars. How did this occur? The secret is in the next few words. "The Lord blessed him" and, the man became rich, and gained more and more until he became very wealthy.

> *…God never intended for man to be without food or abundant provisions. He created everything in abundance.*

I submit to you that God never intended for man to be without food or abundant provisions. He created everything in abundance. If you will study the above passage, you will find that Isaac was in a famine, even a severe economic depression. Yet, through spiritual faith and natural seed, which God indeed blessed, Isaac prospered in a famine, through ordinary farming and faith in God. You'll find that Isaac gained more and more employees, dug wells, and acquired more and more property as you study the scriptures.

Therefore, there is a time to sow unto God, as your faith allows. There also comes a time where God allows the faith-filled you to sow into the land of business and creativity to become naturally blessed, even wealthy, which is in no way a sin but a reflection of the God of abundance. God never intended for us to live in a famine or to barely get by. God is innately abundant and as children made in his likeness, we innately prefer abundance over lack. However, consider this:

At the point that you realize that God's wealth is not solely for you to greedily consume, but to also bless and help others around you, only then will you help position yourself to be supernaturally blessed of God.

Seed is both a natural and spiritual concept. Genesis 8:22 says, *"While the earth remains, seedtime and harvest, cold and heat, summer and winter, day and night, shall not cease."* Our creator designed the concept of the seed to be a perpetual lifestyle, as long as the earth remains. In business terms, if there is no investment, there is no return. Nothing in – nothing out. Since the beginning of creation, there was a garden laid aside for Adam and mankind. The garden was designed as a natural means for Adam and Eve to eat, but since God is a spirit, then everything that he does is spiritual.

So, let's look at the passage with Isaac once again. Genesis 26:12-13.

> *And Isaac sowed in that land and reaped in the same year a hundredfold. The Lord blessed him, 13 and the man became rich, and gained more and more until he became very wealthy.*

> *Sow your talent. Plant your idea. Invest in yourself. Allow it to take root and to grow and flourish.*

As Isaac trusted and had faith in his creator, he sowed real seeds into the ground and the Lord blessed Isaac, so much so that he became rich in a short amount of time – the same year. I am convinced that with faith in God, you can become very successful in your natural endeavors. It is your garden, the seed and replenishment of that seed that the Creator has given you to grow and cultivate provisions and abundant futures.

I believe that God has given every Adam and every Eve a garden of his or her own – a business, an opportunity, an idea, a passion, an invention, a calling, a seed for which to farm. It is up to us to take the seeds that God has given us and sow them, nurture them, water them and allow God to bless them. Sow your talent. Plant your idea. Invest in yourself. Allow it to take root and to grow and flourish.

The tithe or tenth of your income is seed. Your tithe is financial assistance to the Church, the Gospel of Jesus Christ, and perhaps someone in need. You can begin planting your garden today. Who plants a seed and does not expect it to sprout. God is pleased when we sow and reap. It is His designated system of provisions for man, his creation. God is supremely intelligent and already knows what we need.

> *One of the major links to your success is in understanding that you have seed, which must be sown in order to realize your place of provisions, even wealth.*

One of the most powerful items given to man is a seed. Remember that seeds are not to be eaten, but to be released to germinate. The business, the idea, or the investments that are not released to God through faith can never be blessed by God. I am convinced that God never intended for his creation to be a poor and starving creation, but a creation, which has all sufficiency, as is indicative in the wealth of resources in the earth.

There is plentiful water, plentiful oxygen, plentiful fuel, plentiful light, plentiful heat, plentiful everything. Your household likewise should be plentiful. It is simply the plan and intentions of God and especially his children – the Children of Light. One of the major links to your success is in understanding that you have seed, which must be sown in order to realize your place of provisions, even a wealth place, as with Isaac. You have talent, skills, and abilities – seeds in you - resources in you that can be watered, nurtured and grown to move literal mountains.

In fact, this process of productivity, investing and sowing is in no way connected exclusively to those of salvation. *"for he makes his sun rise on the evil and on the good, and sends rain on the righteous and on the unrighteous." Matt 5:45.* Anyone who will work their garden and sow their seeds and talents for a return can be abundantly blessed, even wealthy.

The system of sowing and reaping, as you know, is not reserved exclusively to children of light. It is reserved for anyone in God's creation who is willing to work their own gardens, callings, creativity and generosity.

You have as much opportunity to be wealthy and blessed as anyone else. Sow your gifts and your talents in order to reap an abundant life. As a perpetual lifestyle – Release The Seed – Gather the Harvest!

The following parable of Jesus gives us a glimpse of how God expects us to sow and invest the seeds that God gives us. Consider Mathew 25:

*14"The kingdom of heaven is like a man going on a trip. He called his servants and entrusted some money to them. **15**He gave one man ten thousand dollars, another four thousand dollars, and another two thousand dollars. Each was given money based on his ability. Then the man went on his trip. 16"The one who received ten thousand dollars invested the money at once and doubled his money. **17**The one who had four thousand dollars did the same and also doubled his money. **18**But the one who received two thousand dollars went off, dug a hole in the ground, and hid his master's money.*

*19"After a long time the master of those servants returned and settled accounts with them. **20**The one who received ten thousand dollars brought the additional ten thousand. He said, 'Sir, you gave me ten thousand dollars. I've doubled the amount.' 21"His master replied, 'Good job! You're a good and faithful servant! You proved that you could be trusted with a small amount. I will put you in charge of a large amount. Come and share your master's happiness.'*

22"The one who received four thousand dollars came and said, 'Sir, you gave me four thousand dollars. I've doubled the amount.' 23"His master replied, 'Good job! You're a good and faithful servant! You proved that you could be trusted with a small amount. I will put you in charge of a large amount. Come and share your master's happiness.'

*24"Then the one who received two thousand dollars came and said, 'Sir, I knew that you are a hard person to please. You harvest where you haven't planted and gather where you haven't scattered any seeds. **25** I was afraid. So I hid your two thousand dollars in the ground. Here's your money!'*

*26"His master responded, 'You evil and lazy servant! If you knew that I harvest where I haven't planted and gather where I haven't scattered, **27**then you should have invested my money with the bankers. When I returned, I would have received my money back with interest. **28**Take the two thousand dollars away from him! Give it to the one who has the ten thousand!*

*29To all who have, more will be given, and they will have more than enough. But everything will be taken away from those who don't have much. **30**Throw this useless servant outside into the darkness. People will cry and be in extreme pain there."* GOD'S WORD

James 2:26 also support this story, by informing us that God expects us to couple our faith with actual performance. We must take what we have and invest it; develop it, and grow it. We must take our gifts, our seeds, our abilities and put them to work. Otherwise, God may consider us lazy, even ungodly, and allows us to suffer lack, poverty, crying, pain and everything else that lazy stewards will recieve. The penalties of laziness to the poor steward are as extreme as the rewards of plenty to the faithful steward. The choice is yours and mine. It is up to us to be faithful of God's seeds, talents, gifts, and the generosity that's in our care.

Sowers Vs Eaters

Are you a sower or are you an eater? The Lord gives seed to the sower and bread to the eater. 2 Cor. 9:10. The sower and the eater are two different individuals. The sower has no need for the Lord to provide bread, because their harvest from sowing seed and working their talents provides their bread. The "eater" will not sow, by nature. The eater will not work – to their full potential. In fact, everything that the eater receives is eaten, including their seeds. They eat everything they have and will only ask the Lord for more, more, more. But to the sower, God voluntarily gives them more seed without them having to ask. **For eaters, God must provide bread because the eater does not recognize the means that they have to abundantly provide for themselves through their seed.**

> *The sower has no need for the Lord to provide them bread, because their harvest from sowing seed provides abundant bread.*

Are you a sower or are you an eater? If you are an eater, you'll know because you'll have just enough bread to survive each day. If you're a sower, you'll know because you will always have plenty of seed to sow, plenty seed to give away, plenty of talent to work, plenty of opportunities to partake of. Sowers always prefer to sow first, before they eat or ignore their seed. Sowers will always choose to work before play. Sowers will choose productivity over relaxation. In fact, they will work around the clock if it were physically possible.

> *The Lord desires for His royal children to be sowers, producers, investors, developers, and givers.*

The Lord desires for His children to be sowers, producers, investors, developers, and givers. For this reason, he provides sowers with more and more seed. God loves sowers – and cheerful givers!

A seed-eater consumes more than they produce. The eater will always eat the seed, while the sower would rather sow the seed. Hence, God will usually not give the sower bread. God gives seed to sowers, who will create their own bread. Eaters become beggars. God gives bread to eaters, who does not have the maturity, energy and work ethic to produce wheat (so to speak) and create their own bread.

If you are not a sower, I encourage you to become a sower! For, in the beginning of creation, we were designed to function and live by the seed. There's a familiar proverb that says, "give a man a fish, you feed him for a day, teach a man to fish, he feeds himself for a lifetime". When God gives you seed, He has honored you for a lifetime because seed will infinitely produce more seed, if planted. As a sower, you'll find yourself living in the new system of life and provisions for it. It is apart of God's system of creation. Consider the following two systems:

God's System	Producer	Leader	Lender	Creator	Sower	Giver
World's System	Consumer	Follower	Borrower	Spectator	Eater	Receiver
Biblical Evidence	Prov. 22:29	Matt. 20:27	Deut. 15:6	Prov. 12:24	Gal. 6:7	Acts 20:35

LIFE LESSON 20
10 Principles of Godly Order

Principle 1 God brings form and order in two ways, by his Word and by his Spirit.

Principle 2 Where ever God's spirit hovers (over or around), there will inevitably be light. Light is God's nature. The offspring of God's nature and spirit is Children of Light. Righteousness and light are synonymous with the nature of God.

Jesus, the light of the world, is the express image of God. Heb. 1:3. Moses face shone with light after being in the presence of God.

Principle 3 Whatever the Spirit of God fills, it takes on God's image of identity and order, as it yield to God's spirit.

Principle 4 Where there is no order, chaos is inevitable. Chaos, (Χάος), is a Greek term meaning the lack of order. When life has no set order, boundaries, or structure, life is chaotic, void, and often very dark - unsuccessful.

Principle 5 To increase the order in your life, increase three things: i.) the Spirit of God, ii.) faith in the Word/Law of God and iii.) action based upon God's word. (Adhering to the seeds of tithes is an example of God's order, being a part of household finances).

Principle 6 Unless you bring everything that concerns you under the control of the Spirit of God, your life will be void of form, structure, and peace.

Principle 7 Where there is an absence of the Holy Spirit, the form and structure of one's life will be severely lacking.

Principle 8 As children of light, we have the power to create order in our lives by speaking the powerful Word of God over our lives and over various situations in our lives. As God created universal order and form by speaking "Let there be", we too are to create righteous formation and order into our lives, by praying and declaring God's Word in our homes, careers and overall lives.

Principle 9 Invest 50% of your income into production and 50% into consumption. Man is to live by the growth of the planted seed. Man is to eat the fruit and not the seed. Like any farmer after a harvest, put aside a designated portion of your harvest for re-seeding. Out of any fruit of increase that you receive, you should take at least 20% of the fruit and plant it into God's soil, as seed for continued and sustained provisions – (tithe & charity offerings). Invest or save another 30% in a profitable account for retirement, college funds, etc and consume the remaining 50% for food, shelter, supplies, responsibilities, and taxes. This may call for reducing expenses, debt and other extraneous expenditures in order to increase divine rewards of faith and to create a profitable household based on production and not aggressive consumption.

Principle 10 The church belongs to Jesus Christ, who is the same as the Seed – the Word of God, which was buried in the earth for three days. We are to also plant Jesus Christ (the seed) in our own hearts that He may grow up in us to the point that he is formed in us to bear much fruit, both naturally and spiritually.

THE 5 LEVELS OF FAITH

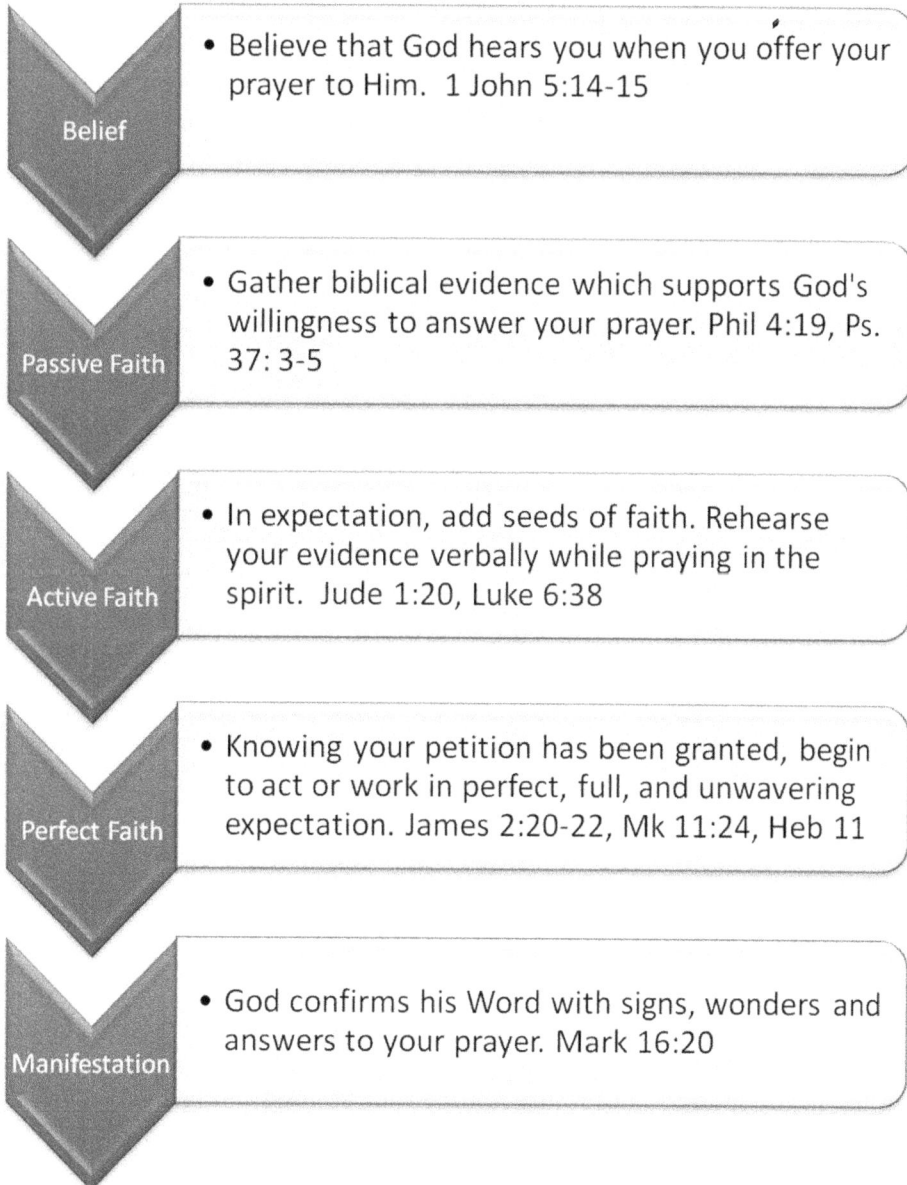

Belief
- Believe that God hears you when you offer your prayer to Him. 1 John 5:14-15

Passive Faith
- Gather biblical evidence which supports God's willingness to answer your prayer. Phil 4:19, Ps. 37: 3-5

Active Faith
- In expectation, add seeds of faith. Rehearse your evidence verbally while praying in the spirit. Jude 1:20, Luke 6:38

Perfect Faith
- Knowing your petition has been granted, begin to act or work in perfect, full, and unwavering expectation. James 2:20-22, Mk 11:24, Heb 11

Manifestation
- God confirms his Word with signs, wonders and answers to your prayer. Mark 16:20

You're Invited

Without faith, it is impossible to please God." (Heb.11:6) God expects everything we do to include faith - everything. "That which is not of faith is sin." (Rom. 14:23) Never forget this biblical quote; it is very important. What that means is that our entire lives should be guided by our faith, God's plan and order for humanity. Everything that we do in life can be guided by faith in our Creator's plan for successful living. This may be difficult to understand, unless you see things the way God sees things. Allow me to explain a little further.

God made the universe, heaven, earth, man, woman, vegetation and everything that pertains to life. God created Adam's first occupation. God gave man wisdom to live and to be sustained through knowledge and productivity. However, although man has largely forgotten God and often chooses to live life apart from God, there is a divine order, a plan, a policy manual, a law that we often ignore. It's called the Holy Bible.

> *Everything we do in life should be guided by faith in our Creator's plan for successful living.*

The concepts of the bible is the "faith" – in which we live by. Our "faith", which is listed in the Bible, details how we should live our lives. "The righteous shall live by faith", the bible says in Hebrews 10:38. So once again, any lifestyle that is misaligned with your faith is in error because God's children are to live by their faith – a belief system based in God's Word, power and provisions.

Some may ask, "Why can't I just live my own life the way I want; why does everyone talk about sin, as if they are perfect, when God doesn't want me to be miserable." I respond to statements of that nature in this way. God doesn't want any of us to be miserable. That's why he gave us instructions to prevent us from having a miserable life. Often, we feel inclined to live life a certain way, only to realize that serious mistakes and penalties must be paid later in life for failure to heed Godly order and instructions. Our biblical instructions are not for God. These instructions are for our benefit.

> *........"God left instructions for you to live a wholesome, fulfilled, and successful life".*

Now, God will allow you to do anything that you want to do – good or bad. You can try anything you want to try; experience anything you want to experience. God loves you so much that he granted you complete freewill – ultimate freedom to choose. To ORDER you to obey and love Him, would only make you a robot that responds to orders, having no heart to respond to Him with love, commitment, or voluntary obedience. God gave us the curse and blessing of freedom. We have the wonderful blessing to create new life. But, we also have the ability to destroy life, even our own. Many lives are destroyed as a result or riotous living, drugs, murder, suicide, war, hurt, malice, greed, and poverty. Freewill can take your life, but freewill can also save your life eternally.

God left instructions for us to live a wholesome, fulfilled, and successful life.

To have complete and well-rounded success in life, you must have faith in God. Without faith, you're a floating un-anchored meteor headed for an eternal collision. It's just a matter of time.

God always sends warning before destruction. Remember those red exit signs on the inner door of a building that says, "Do Not Exit" or alarm will sound. Ponder the sound of a smoke alarm in the middle of the night? It's a LOUD warning to get your attention. That's what this book may be for you. It may be a warning siren to get your attention.

I pray and plead with you to "stop" "STOP", right now and consider your faith and the importance of it. **It's Time!**

Are you living by faith?

If you are, that's wonderful. But, there's always room for improvement, right? Look for ways to increase and perfect your faith. If you're not living by faith, I invite you to establish your faith and peace with God, through living by the teachings of Jesus Christ.

You can establish your faith right now by confessing Jesus Christ as your Lord and Savior. God sent his son to redeem man from the eternal train wreck of life.

If you're not living by faith, I invite you to establish your faith and peace with God, through living by the teachings of Jesus Christ.

You must begin living life by faith in Him. I have one more question for you.

Did Jesus pay the penalties for your disobediences to God in vain?

Don't allow the crucifixion of Christ to be in vain in your life. Turn from living life apart from God and apart from faith and accept a life of peace, harmony, and happiness with God. A major component of Success In Life is having peace with God, your Creator.

God has no intention of stealing life or success from you. He made it all. Instead, He is trying to get a better life of success to you. God wants you to enjoy life. I want you to enjoy life. That's my personal vision in life – helping you enjoy life. This brief tour here on earth is nothing. It's but a moment in the eternity of time. Heaven is a wonderful dimension of life that we cannot imagine. If you think this life has goodness to enjoy. Life in heaven with God will be many many times better.

However, there's a caveat – one major requirement. If you'll have no part of the Father here on earth, then He knows that you won't appreciate being with Him while in heaven either. The fallen Angel Lucifer proved that.

Please understand that God loves you and has already paid an enormous price in blood for you to return to him right now and forever.

Please understand that God loves you and has already paid an enormous price in blood for you to return to him right now and forever.

He's prepared a place for you in heaven, but he also has a wonderful life for you right here on earth, as long as you will live life the Father's way and not your own way. But still, it's your choice.

One of the most important instructions of this book is that you surrender your life to God's plan. That is my sincere recommendation. Now, out of sincerity for your faith, find a place where you can talk to God within yourself. God is an omni-present spirit; He's everywhere, all at the same time. He's near you and He hears, knows and understands your deepest thoughts. He's quite amazing. Find a quiet place alone, in a park, in your room, or any quiet place of serenity and talk to God and tell him how much you really want to love him and appreciate him in return, as he, your father, loved you first. Then as quickly as you can, make your way to a church that teaches the faith and love of Jesus Christ.

Now, for my special invitation,

I invite you to make Jesus Christ the Lord of your life.
I now invite you to lead your family to Success In Life, through Jesus Christ.
I invite you to join my community, so that we can share our experiences of Success In Life through God's plan for our lives.
I invite you to send me an email or write me a letter about your experiences with your faith and with this book.

Until we meet again, may God richly bless you and yours with unimaginable Success In Life! There's nothing that can stop you. This is your moment. This period in history has paused and is awaiting your decision to change the course of your family's destiny. **It's Time.**

Author's Biography

<u>Joseph (Joe) McDaniel, Jr.</u>
Executive Director, Success In Life Ministries, Inc.
Author / Speaker / Consultant / Entrepreneur

<u>Research Interests & Expertise</u>
Life and Purpose
Faith & Philosophy
Socioeconomic Development
Family Entrepreneurship
Business Strategy
Leadership and Change

Joe McDaniel, B.S., M.Ed., MBA is the Executive Director of Success In Life Ministries, Inc. where they provide keynote speaking, consulting, family training and leadership coaching services. Joe currently serves as supporting faculty for the School of Business at the University of North Carolina Pembroke, his Alma Mata, and has been a higher education professional and trainer for more than a decade. Joe received his graduate degrees from Regent University and his leadership training through the John Maxwell Team. Joe is a leadership trainer, conference and motivational speaker, having been personally trained by America's top speaker, Les Brown. As an entrepreneur, minister, military veteran, and 20-year marital veteran to LaTisha Jordan McDaniel, Joe works diligently to see that his four sons, students and clients have the tools they need to live the life they were born to live.

For Booking and workbook materials,
> **please call** 3476 TRY-SIL or
> **please email** joe.mcdaniel@me.com
> **please facebook** www.facebook.com/joe.mcdaniel.jr

www.ingramcontent.com/pod-product-compliance
Lightning Source LLC
Chambersburg PA
CBHW062045090426
42740CB00016B/3027